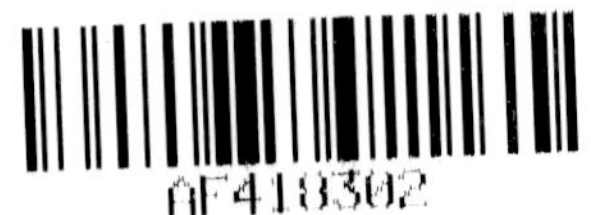

Birthday Art Designs For Relaxation And Mindfulness

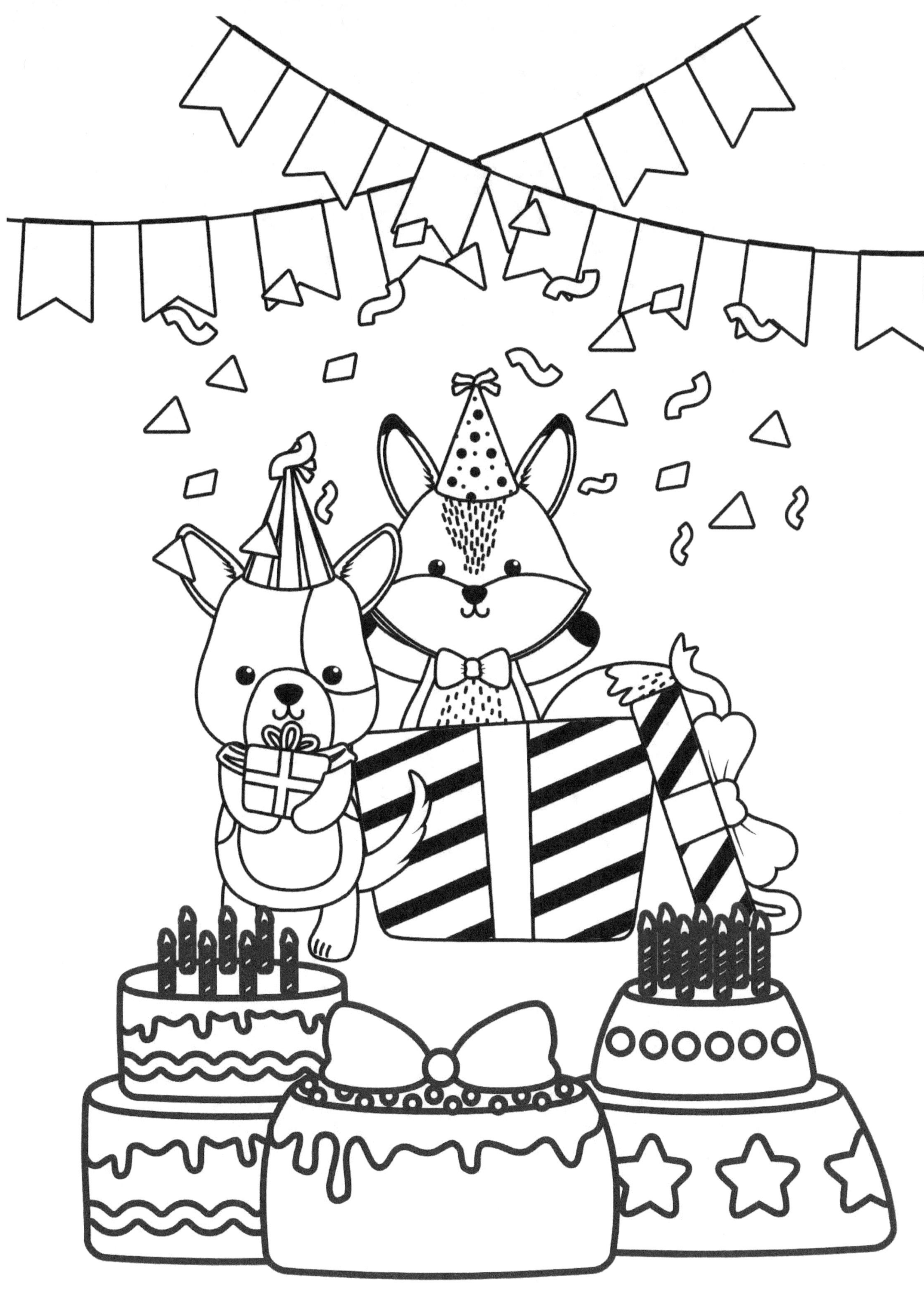

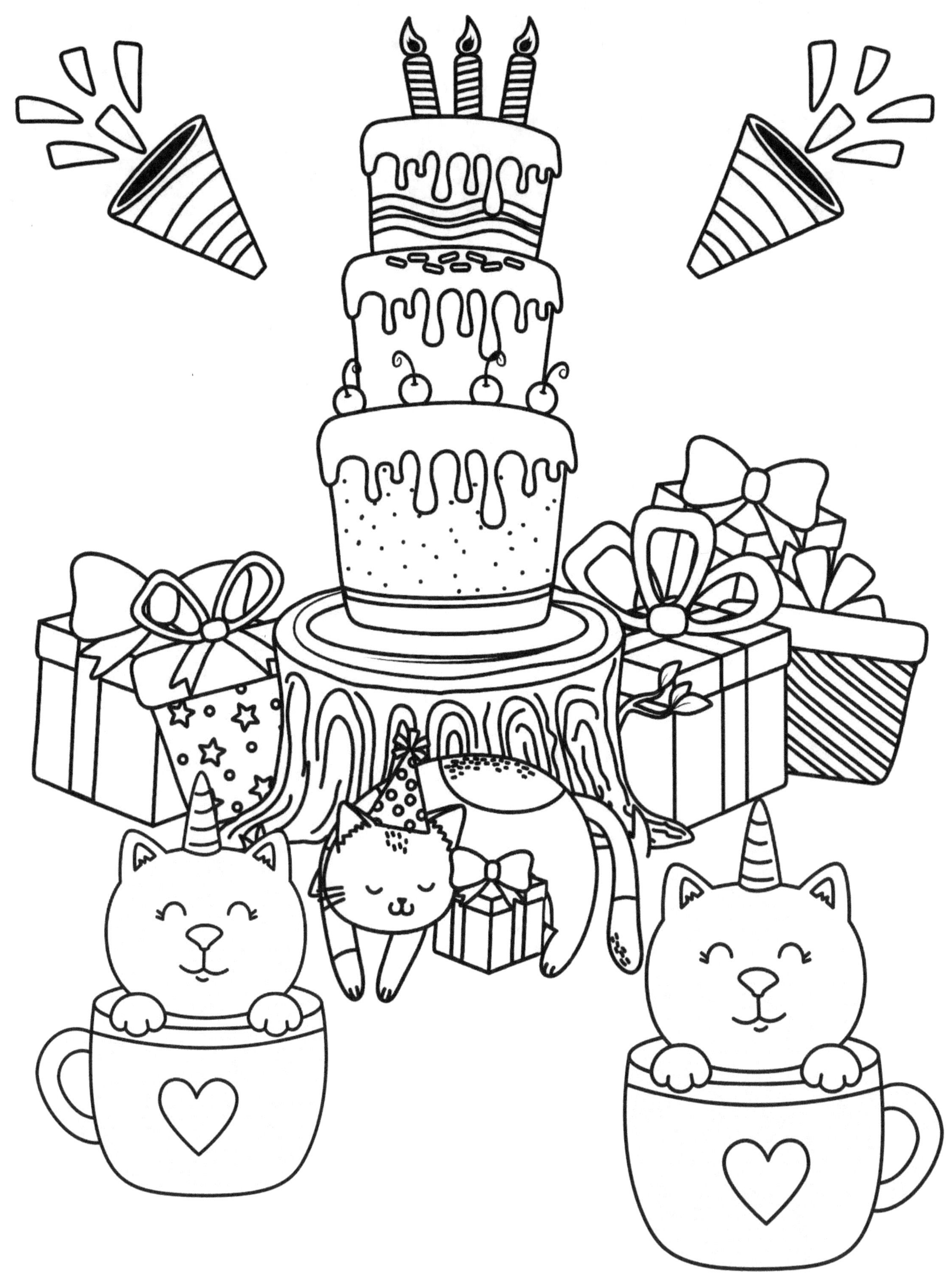

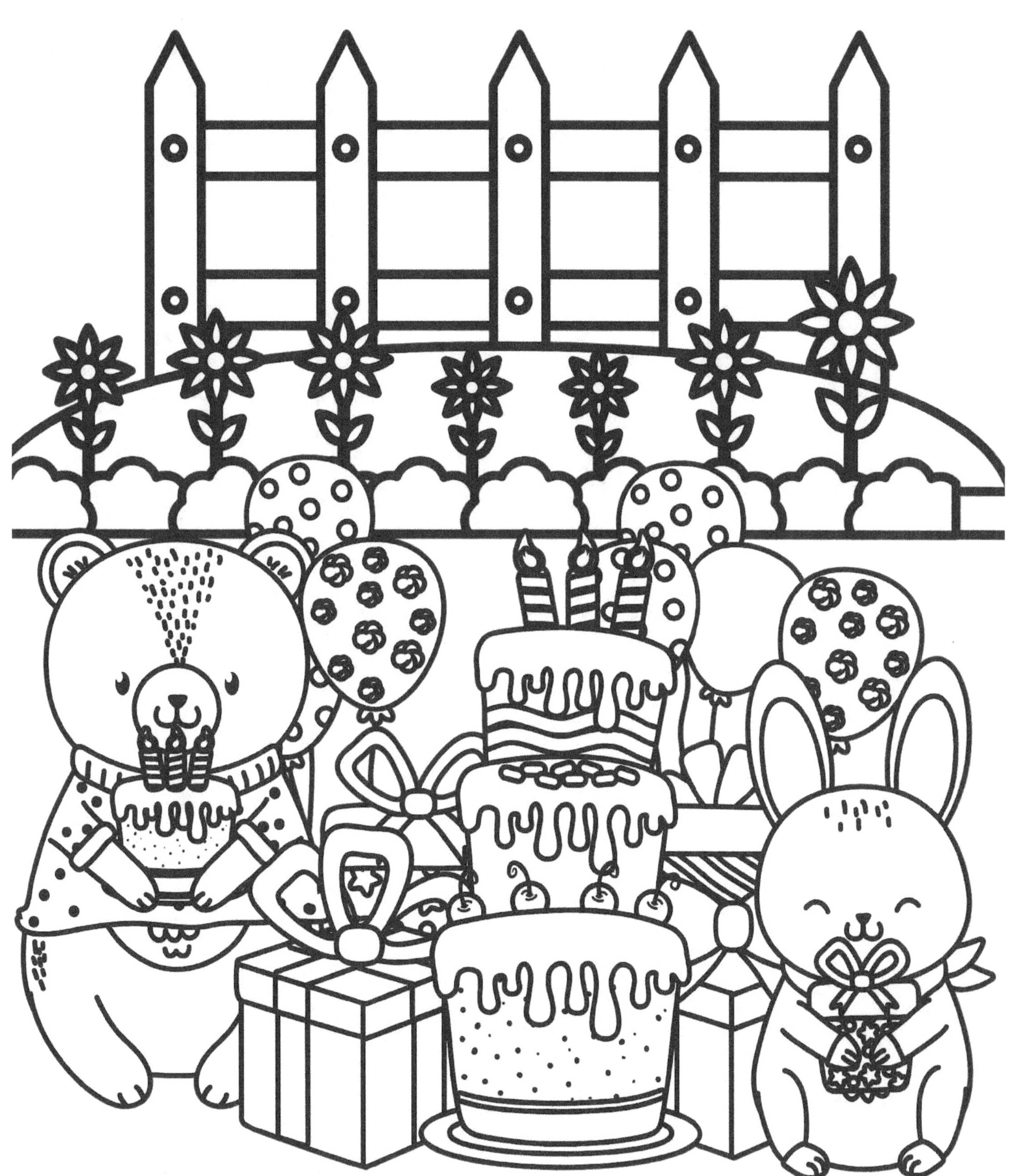

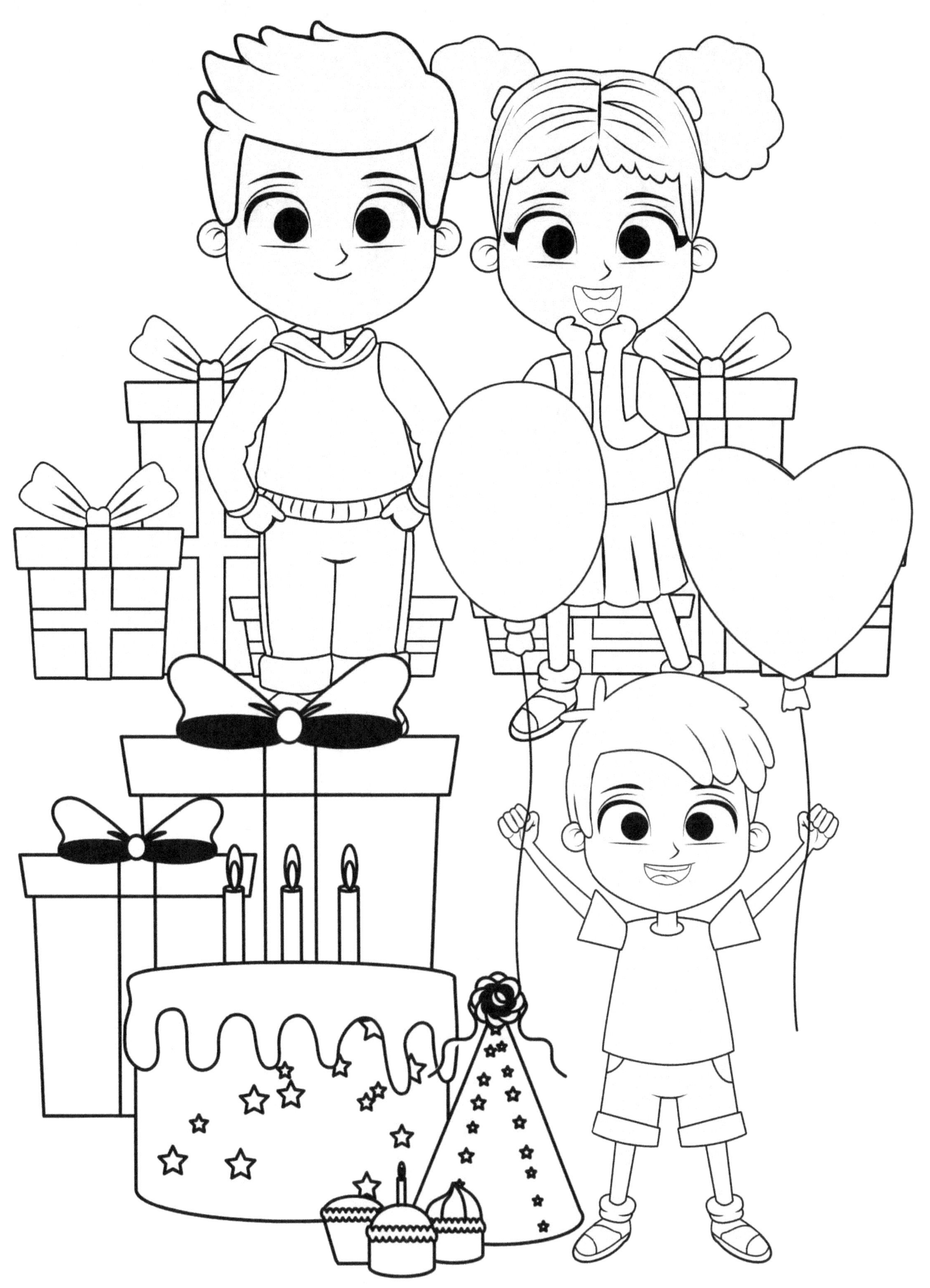

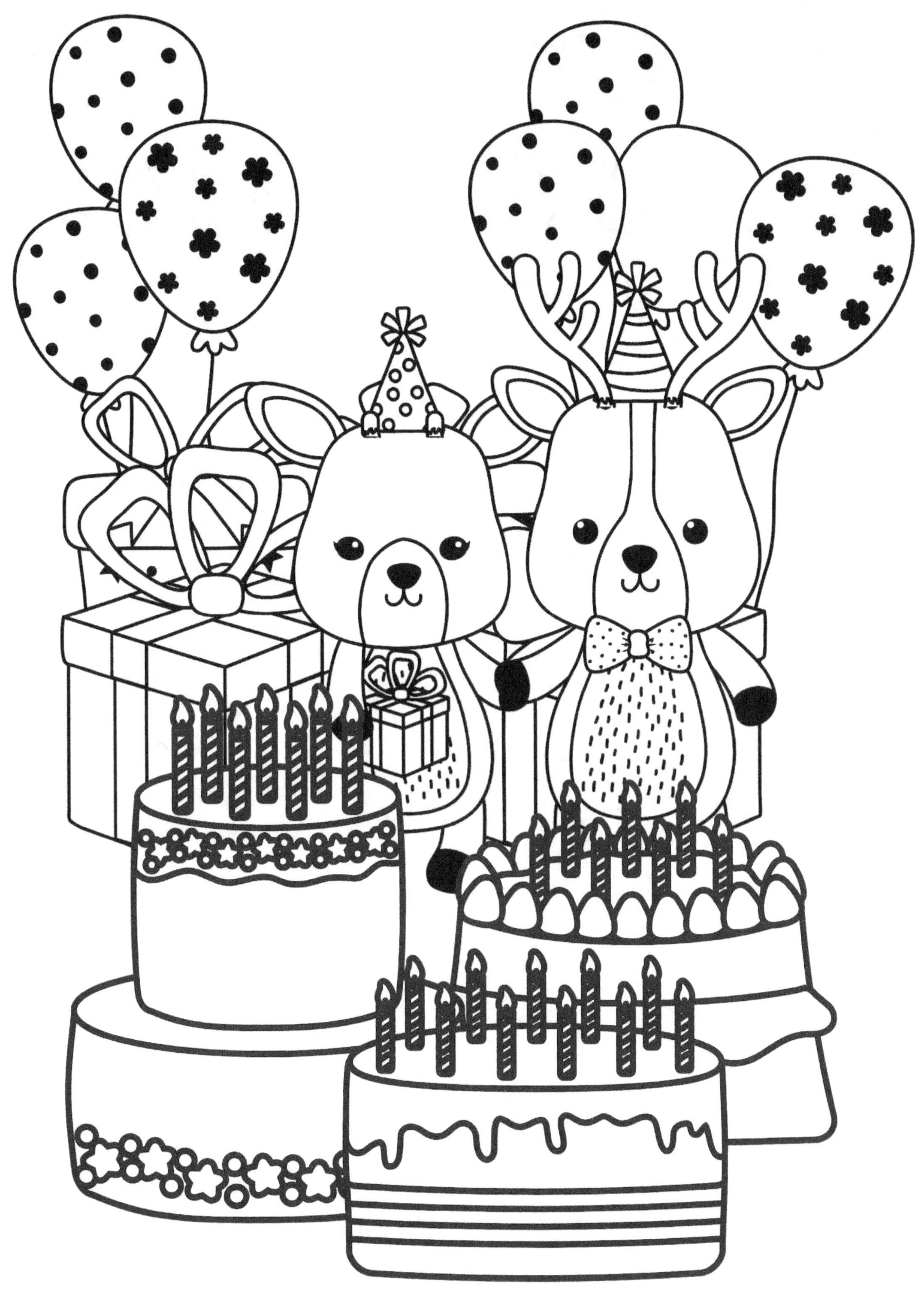

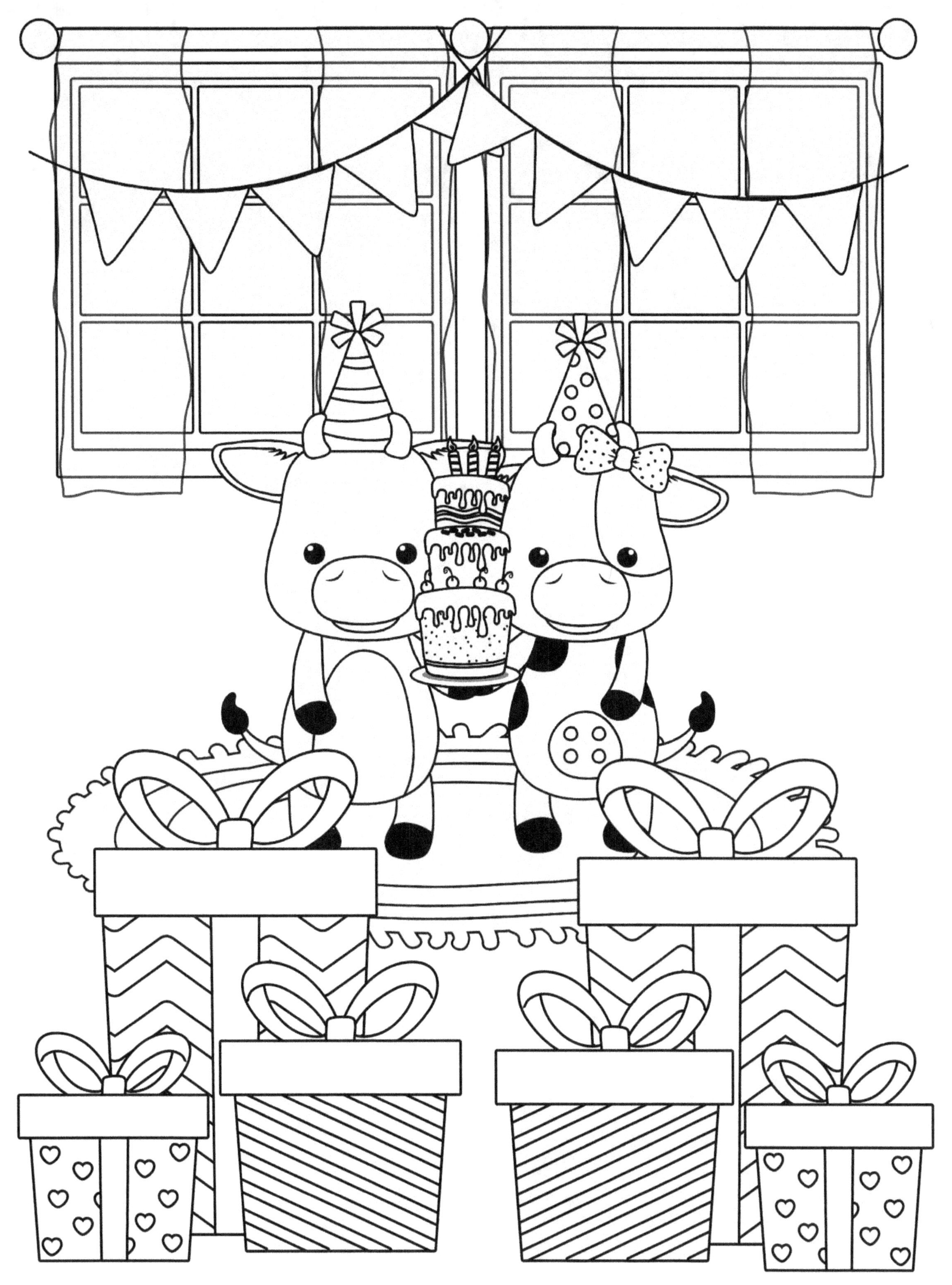

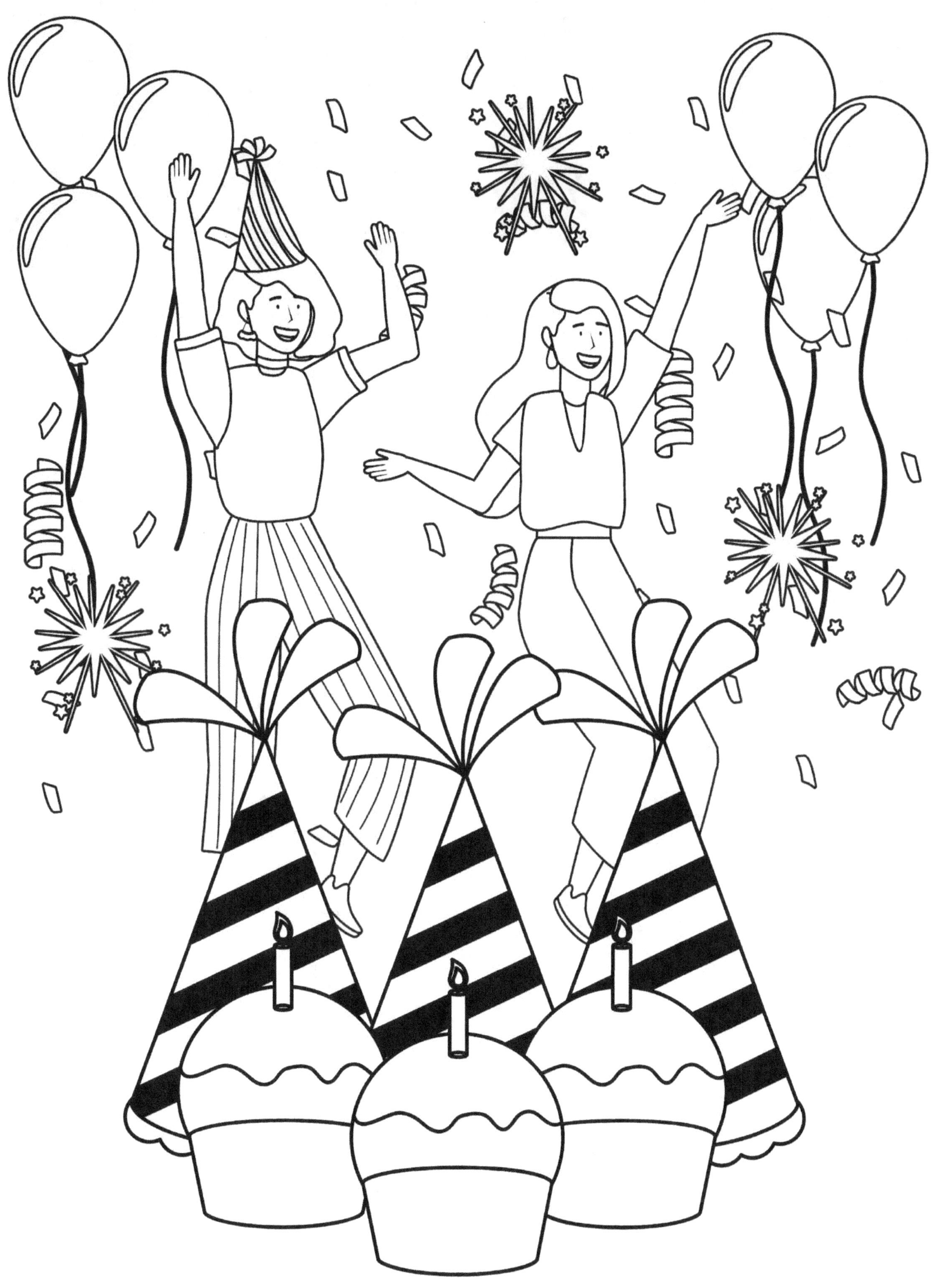

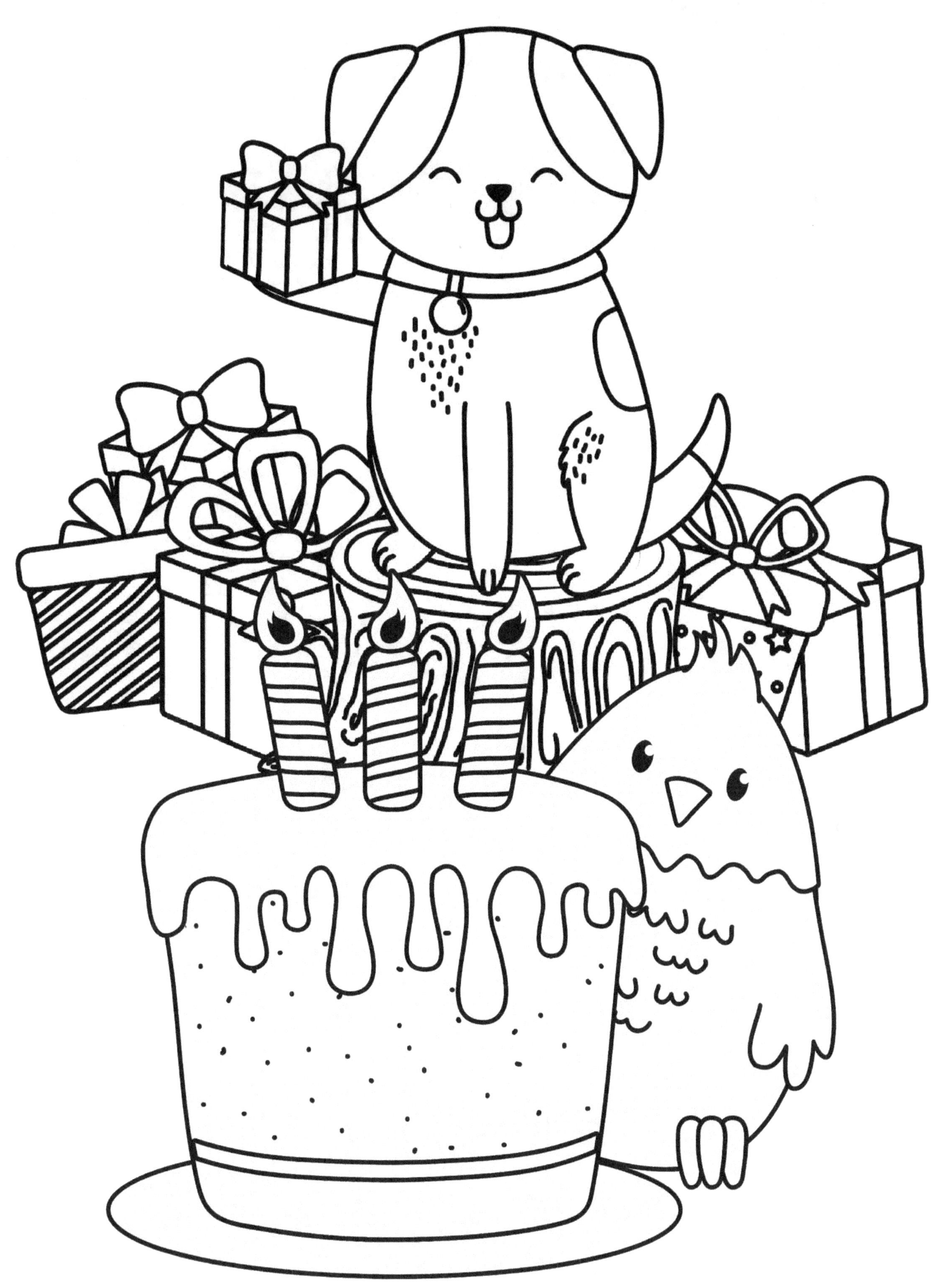

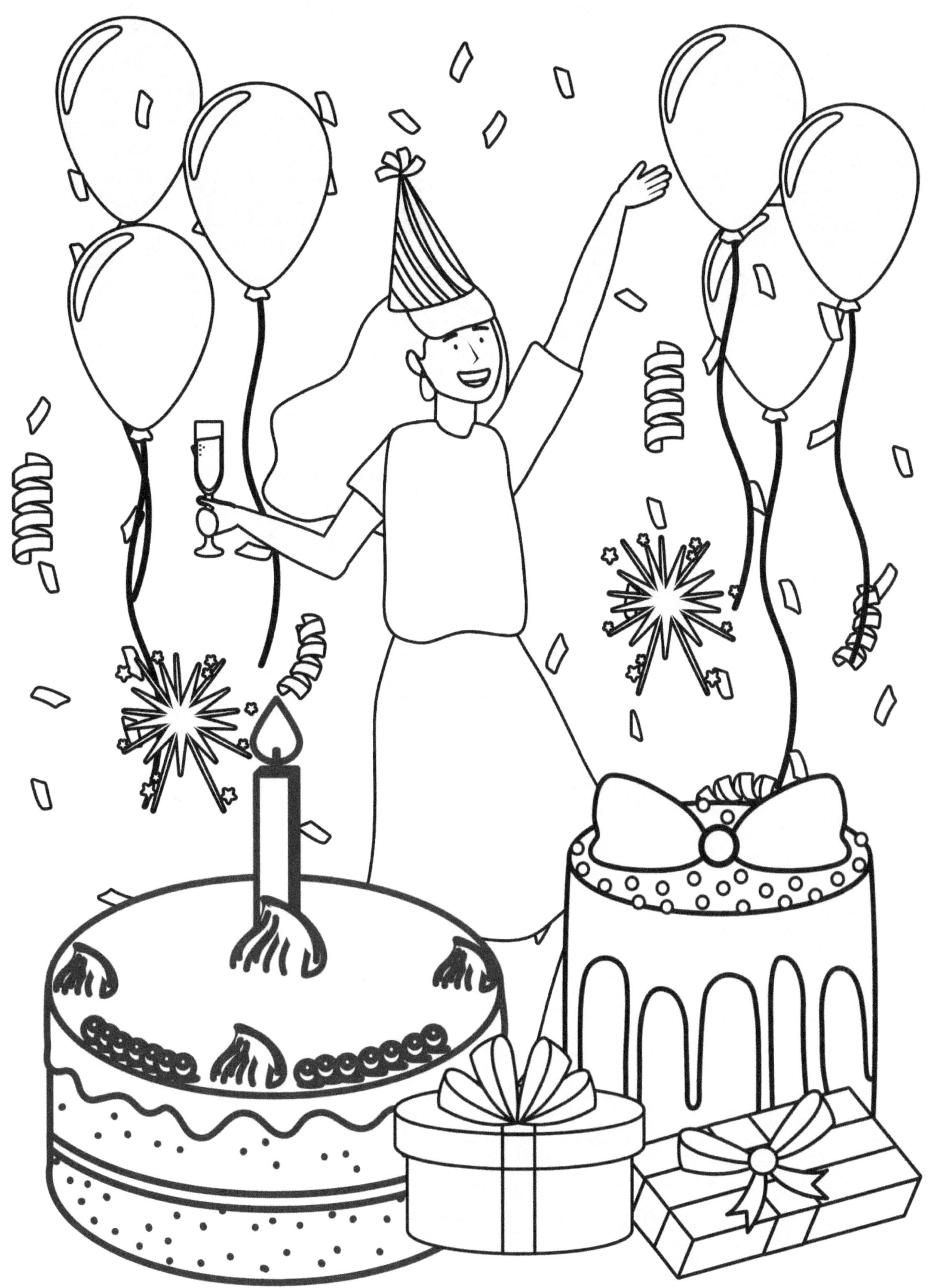

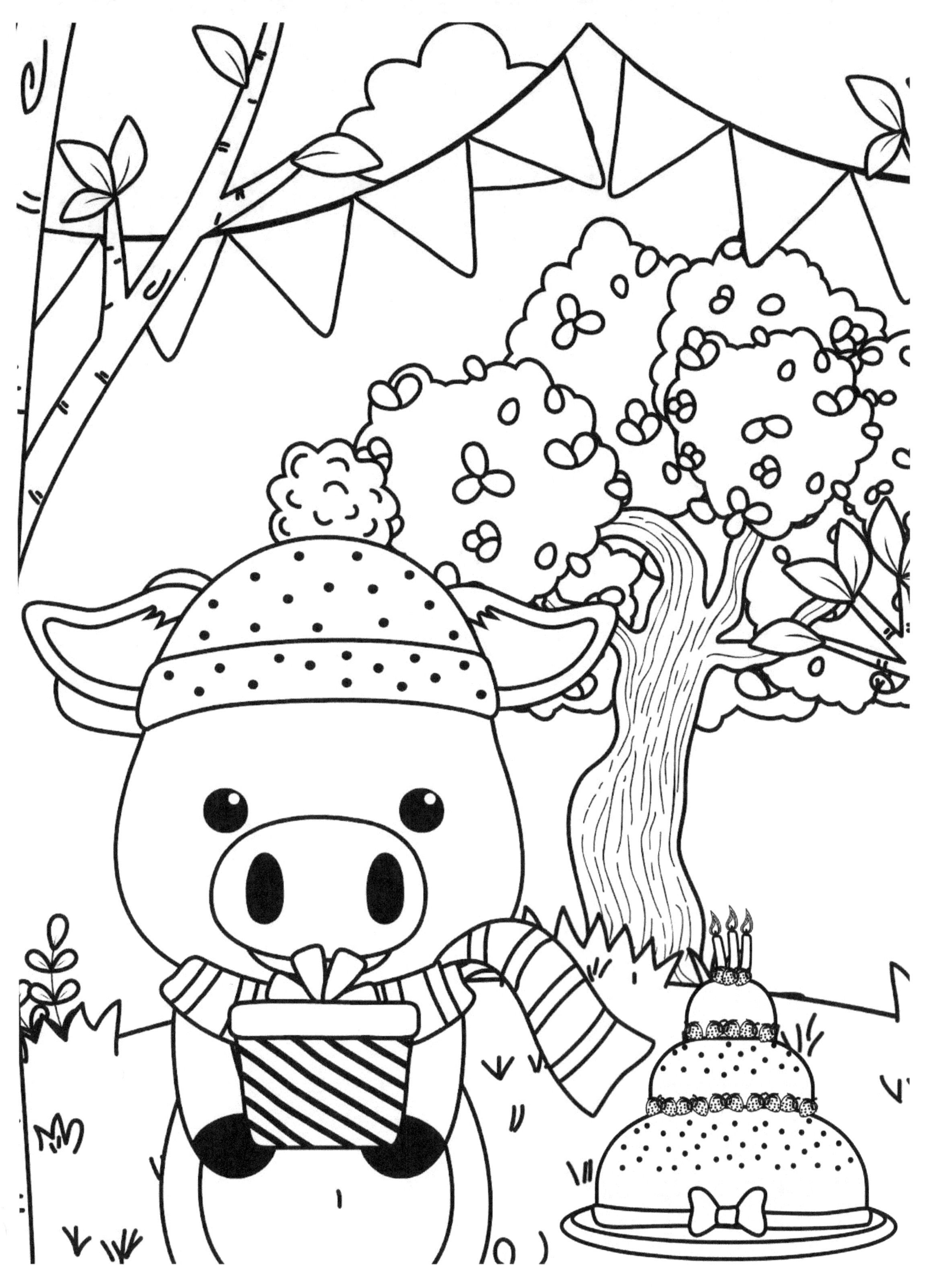

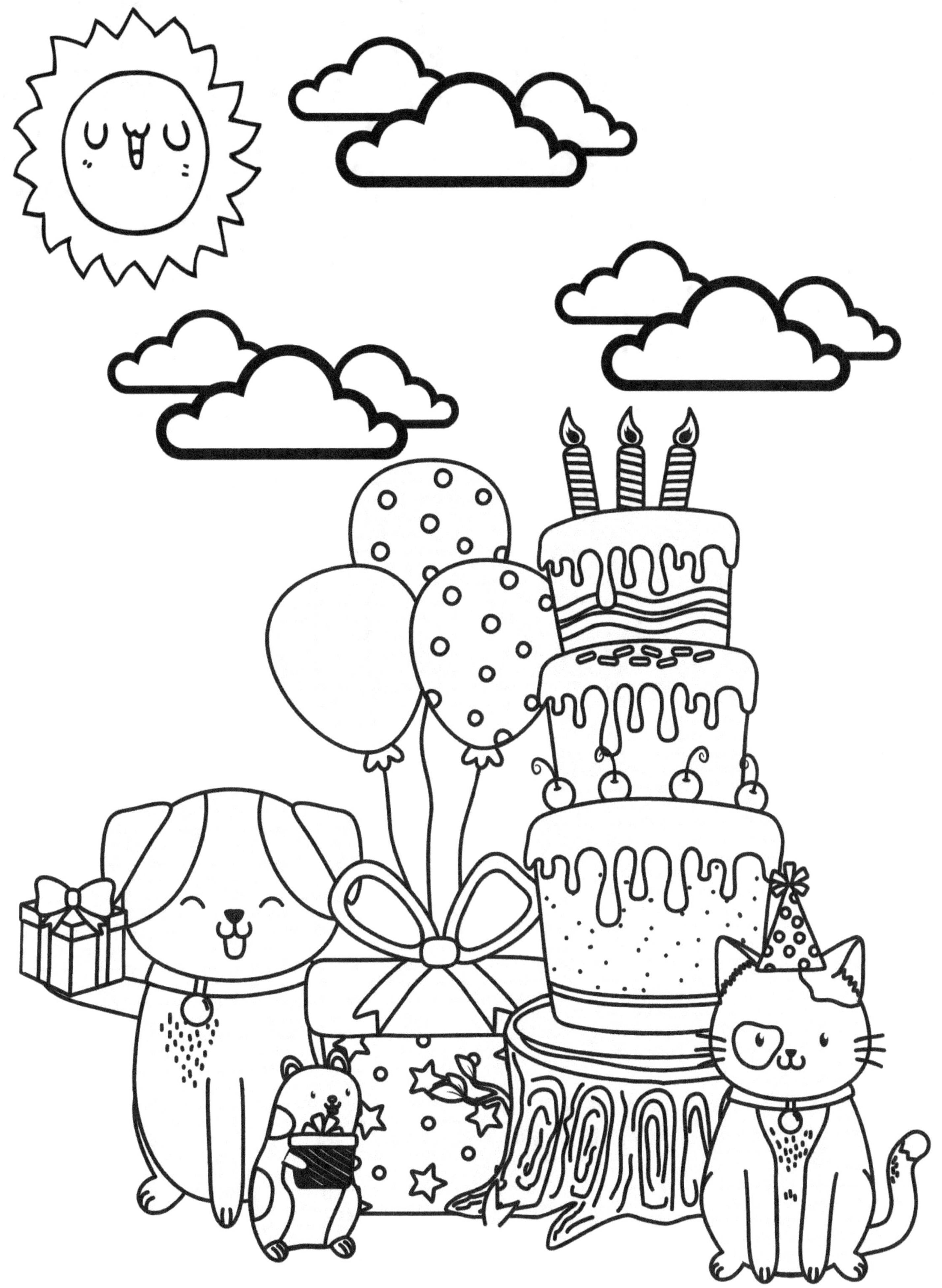

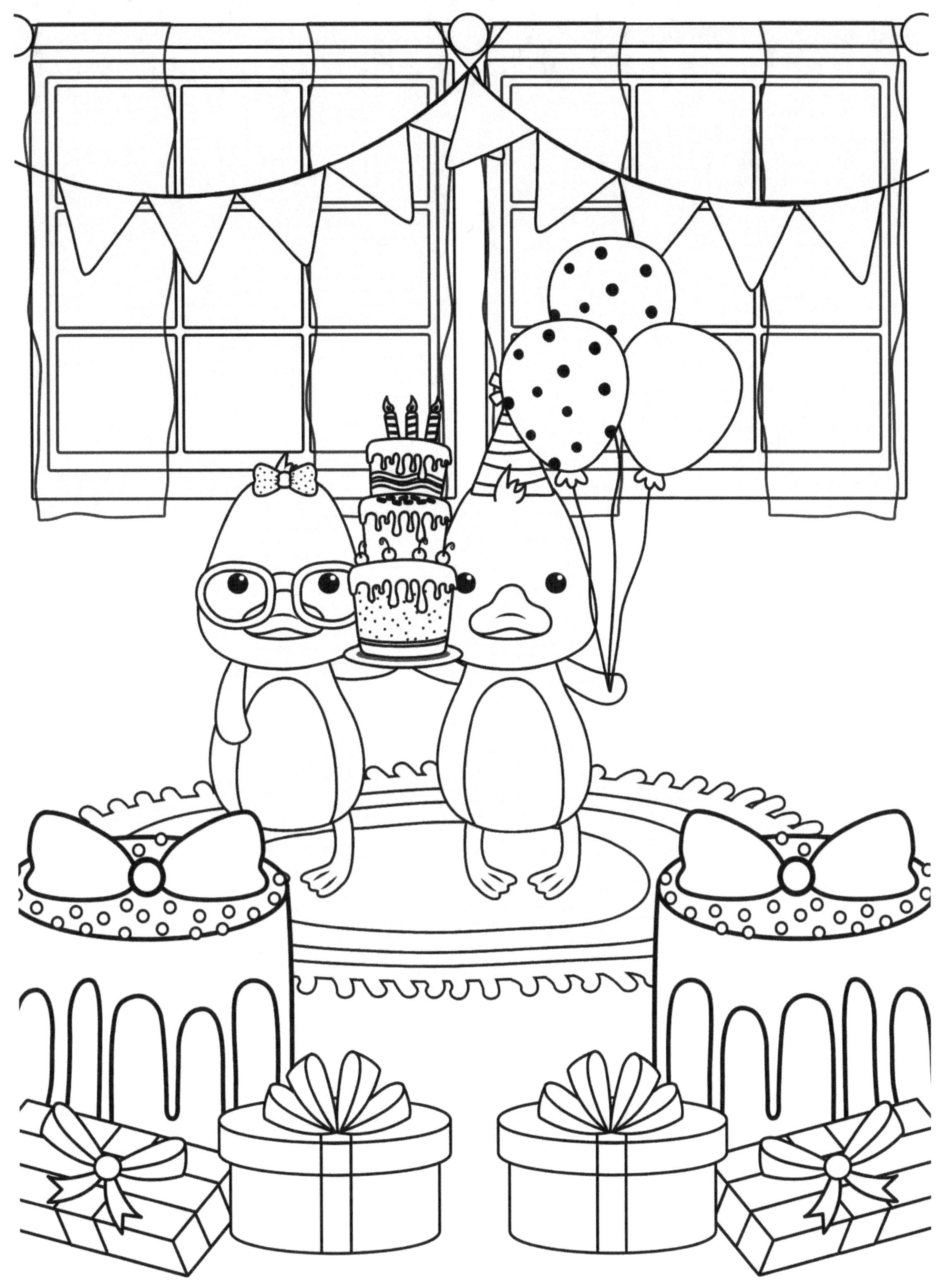

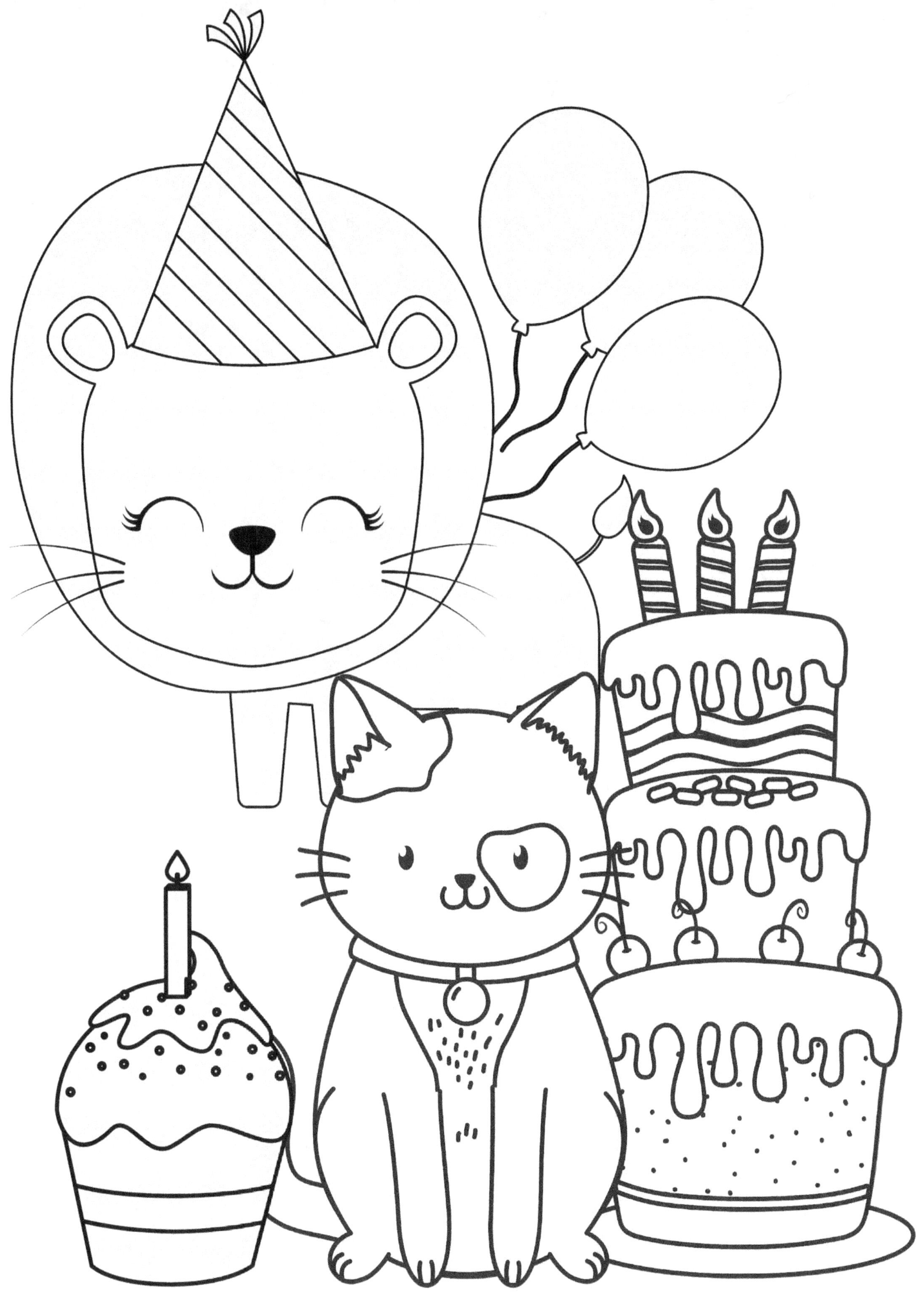

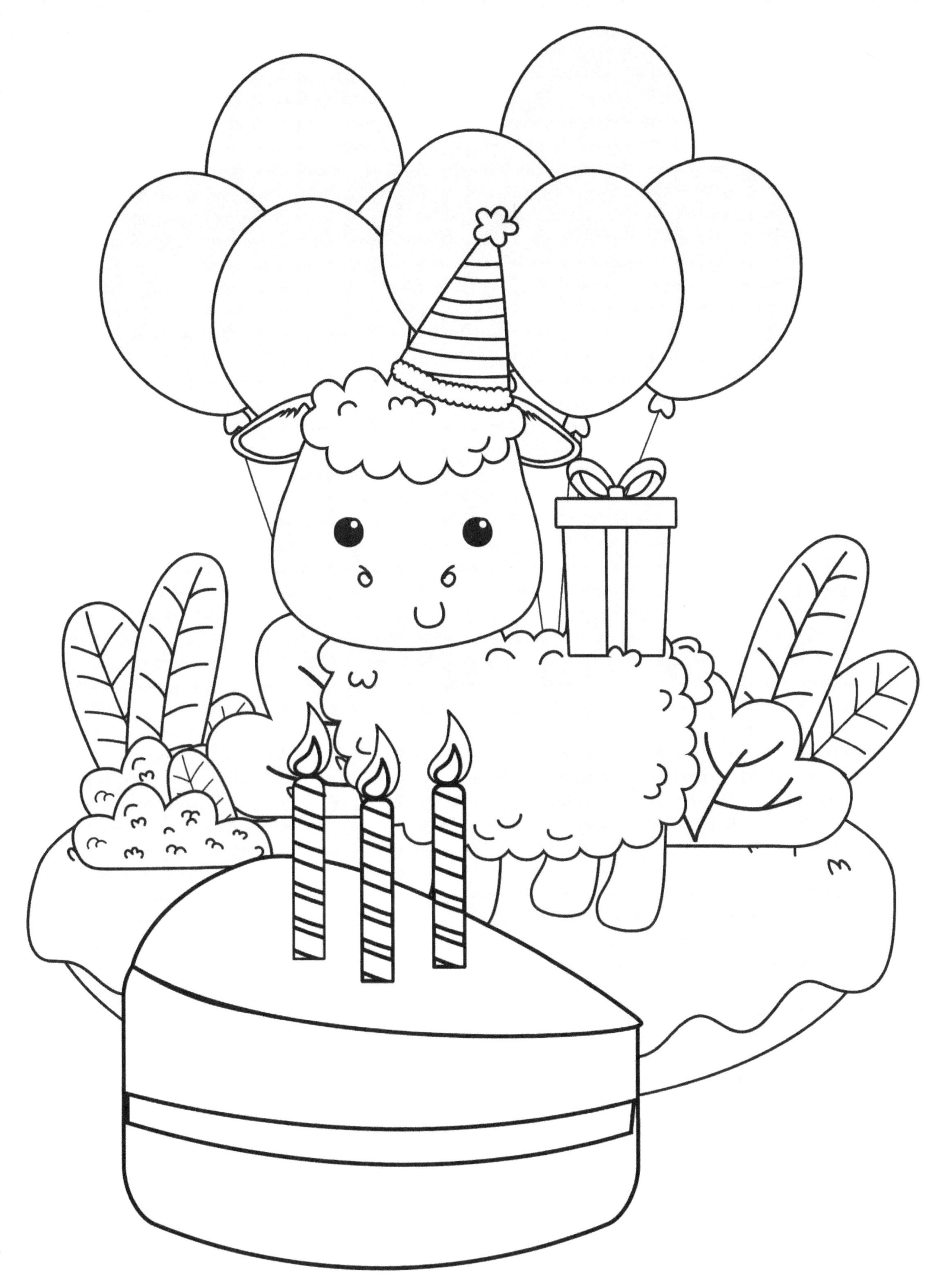

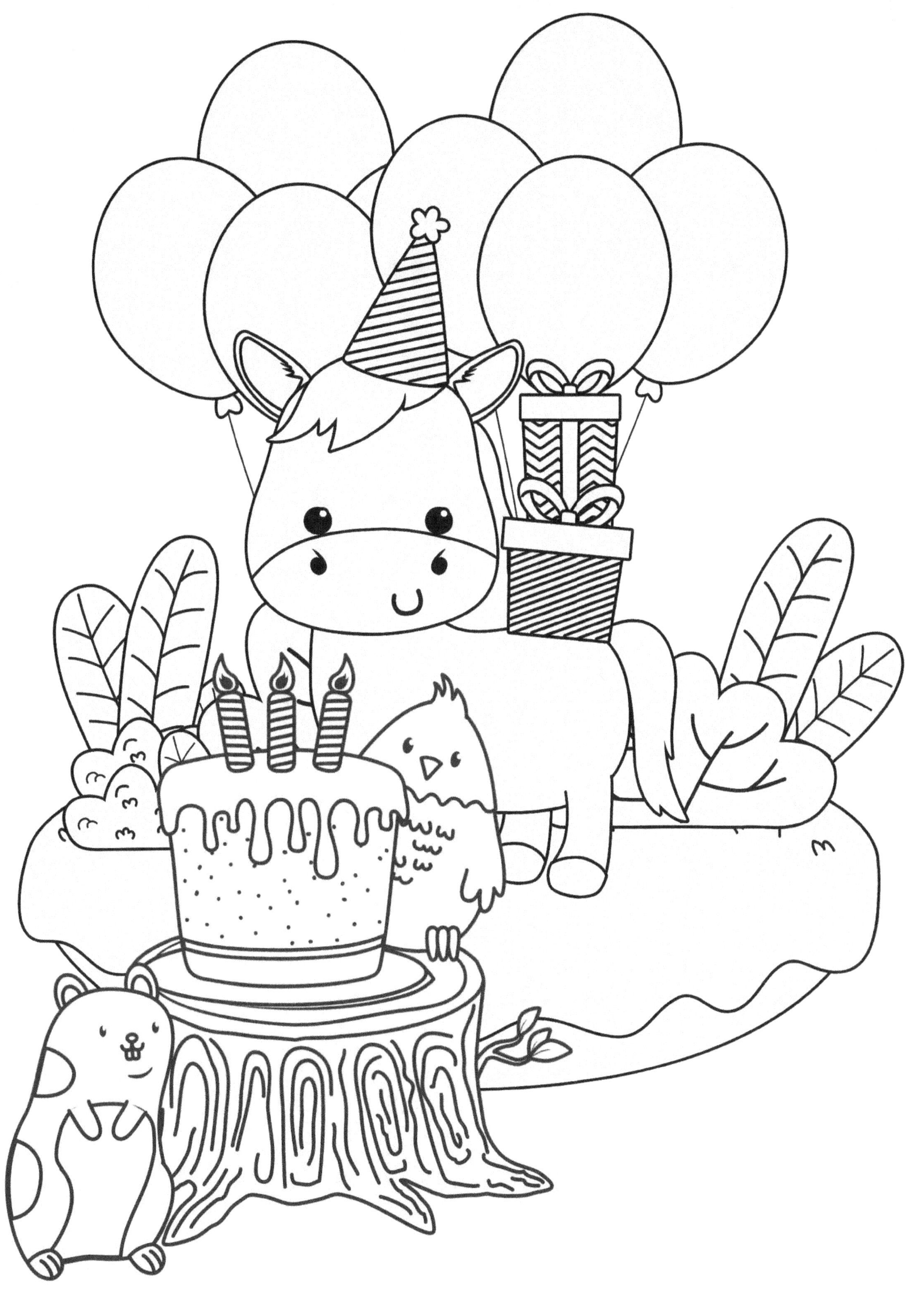

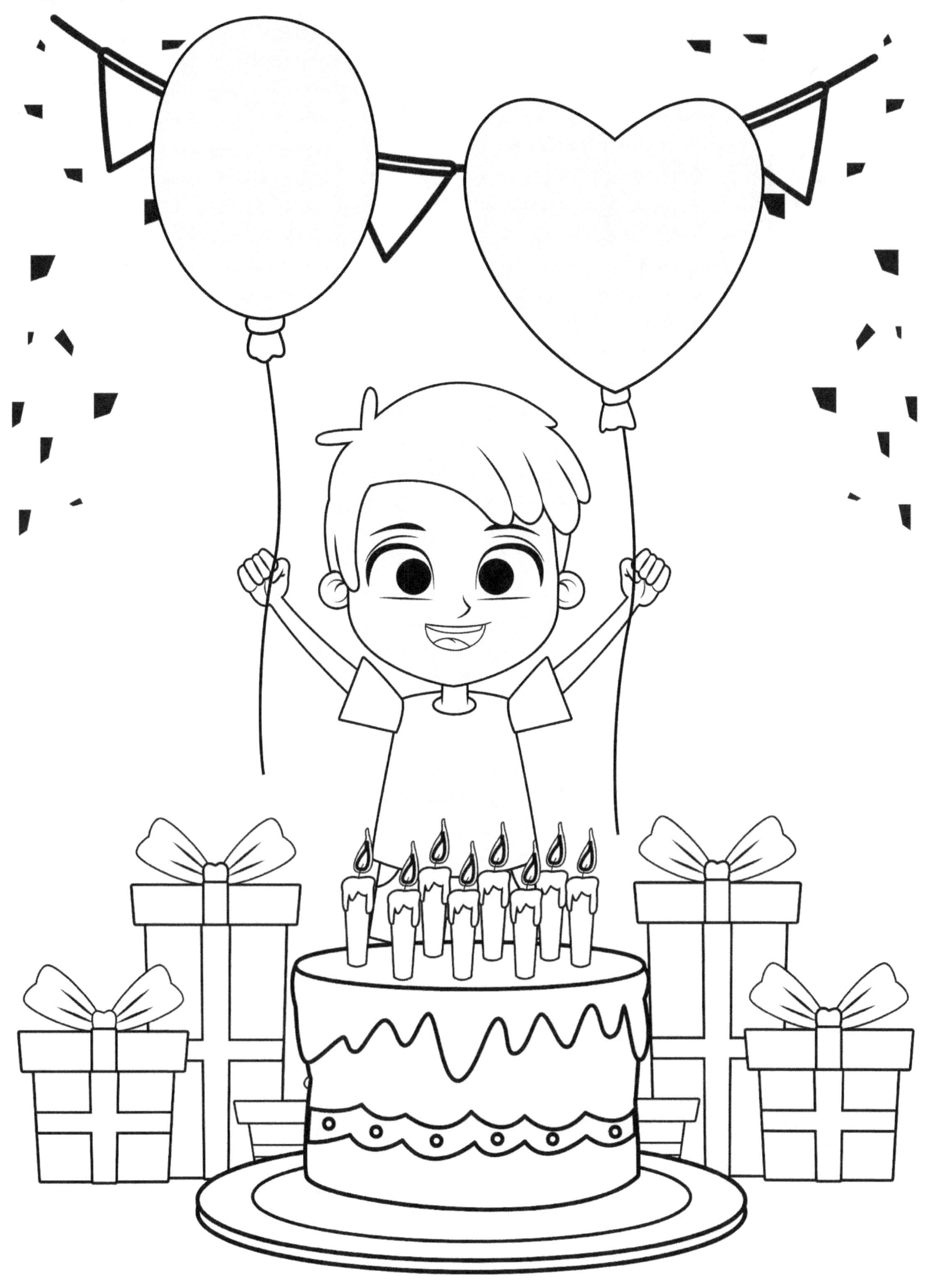

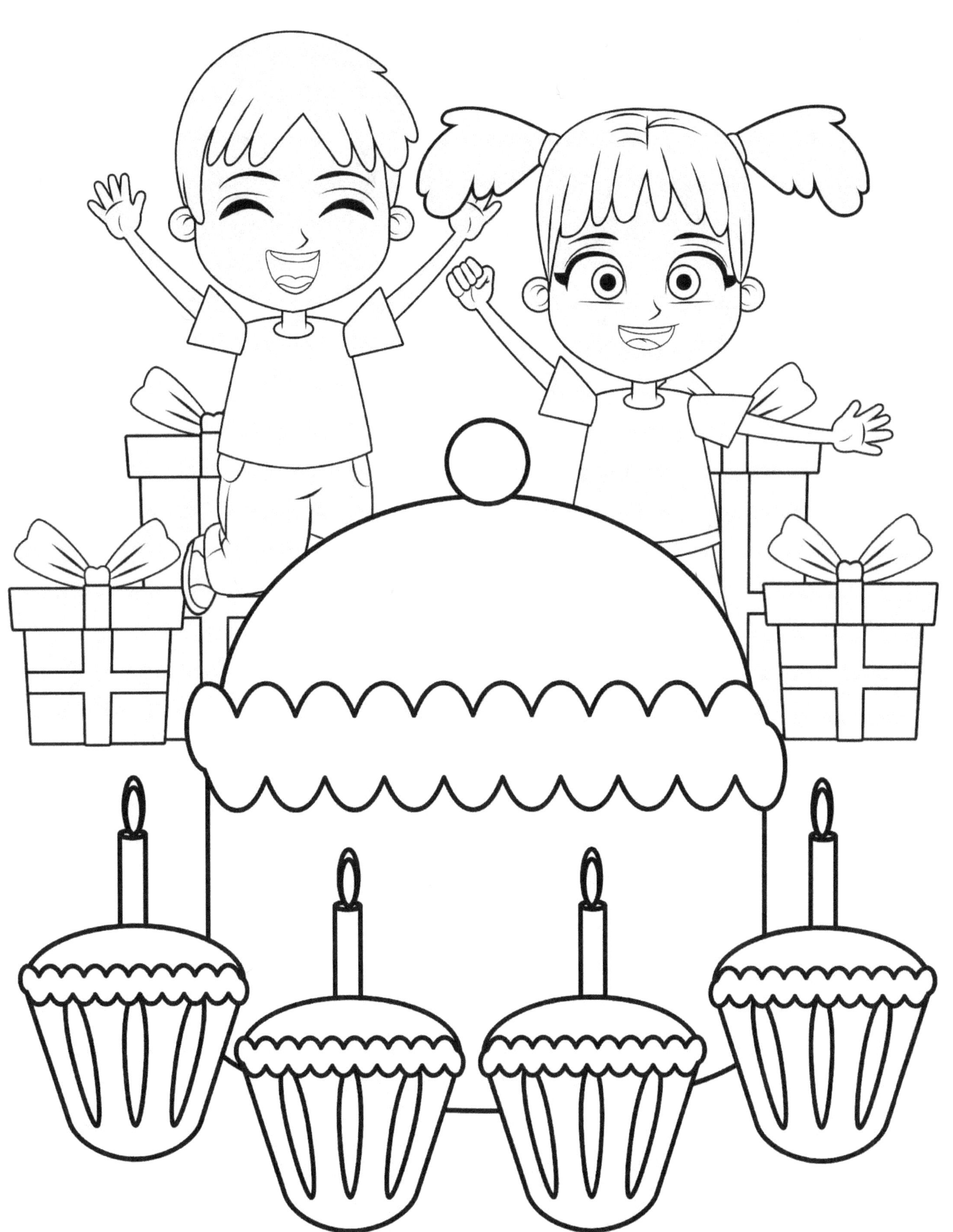

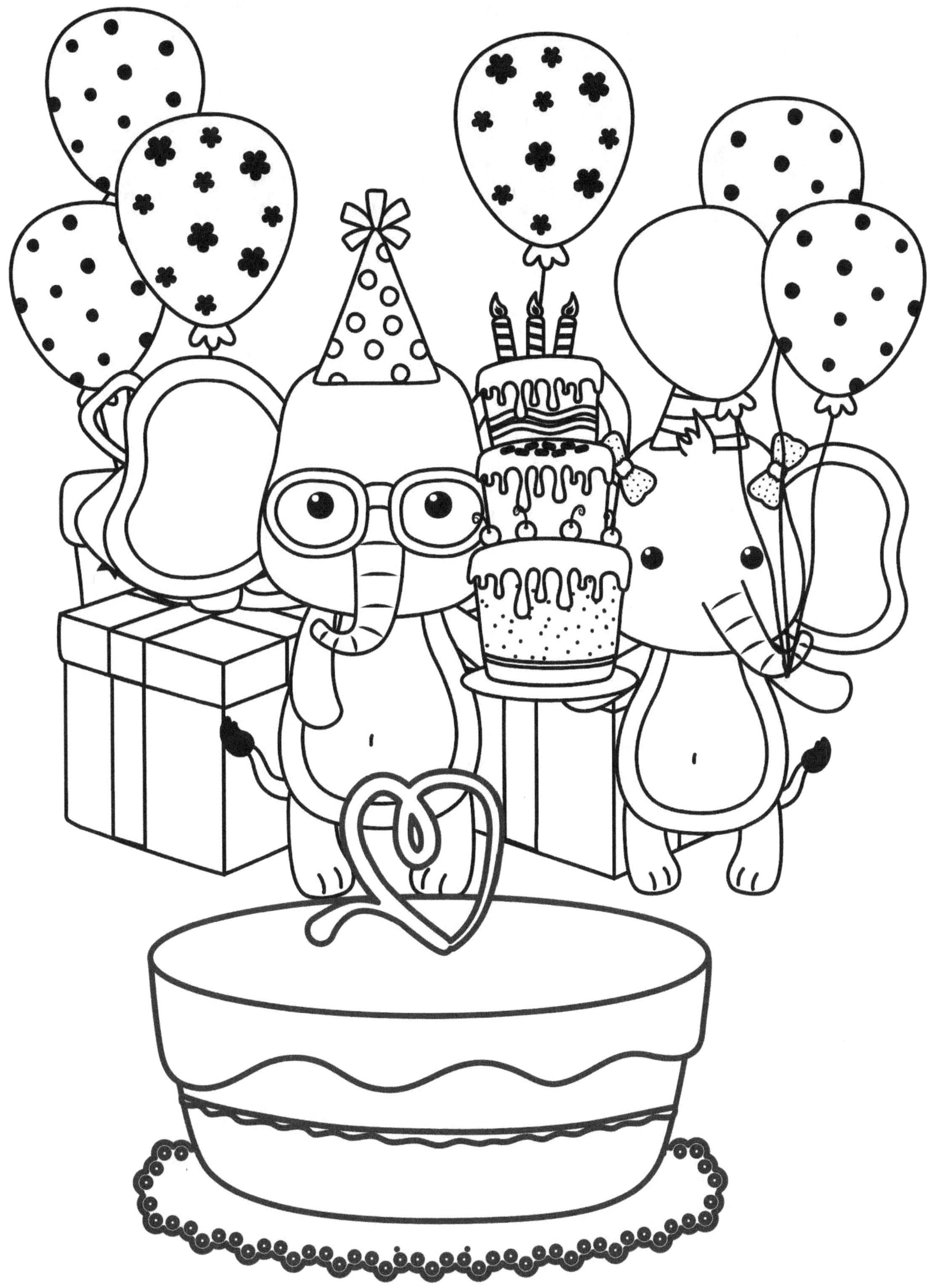

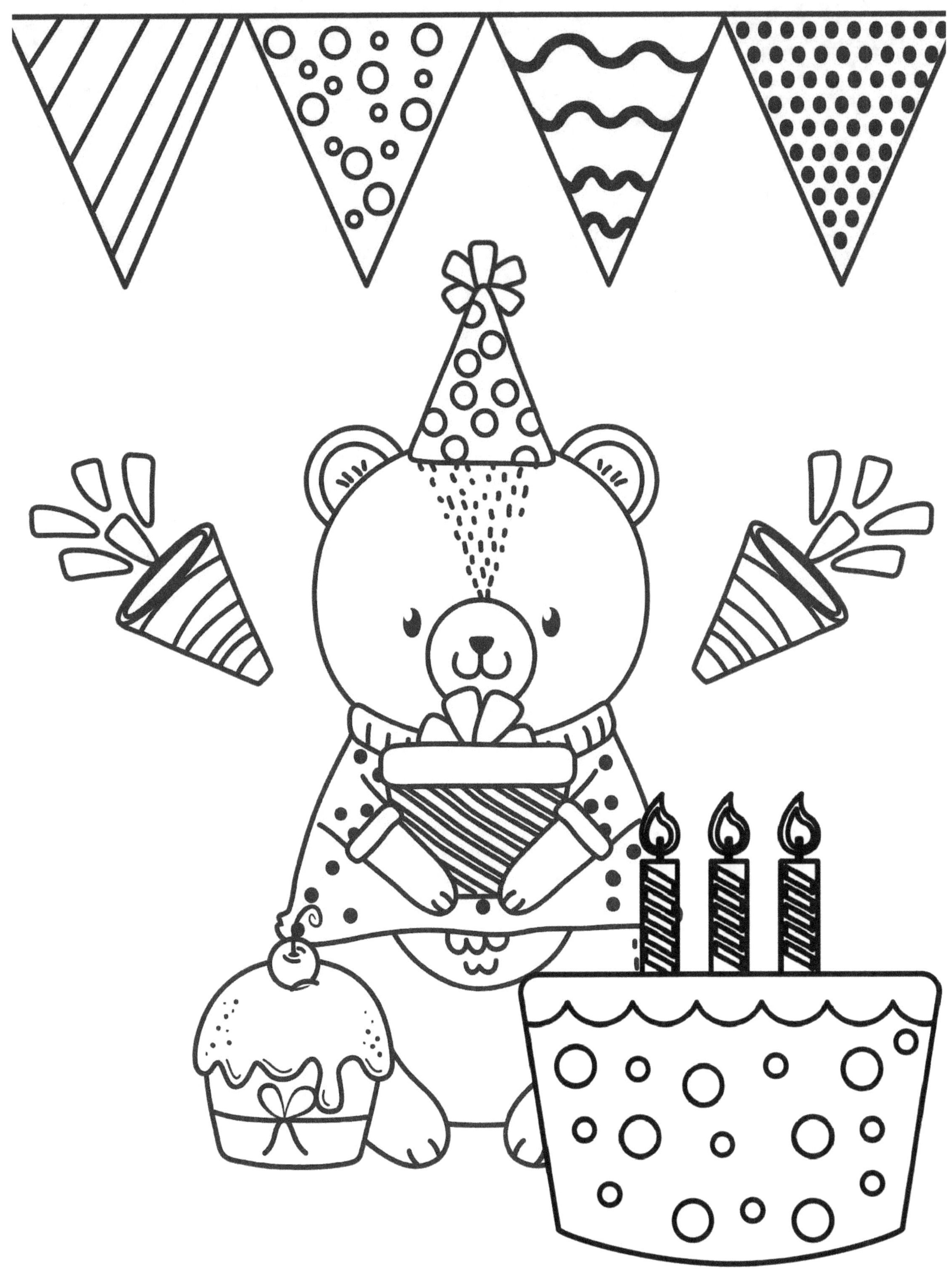

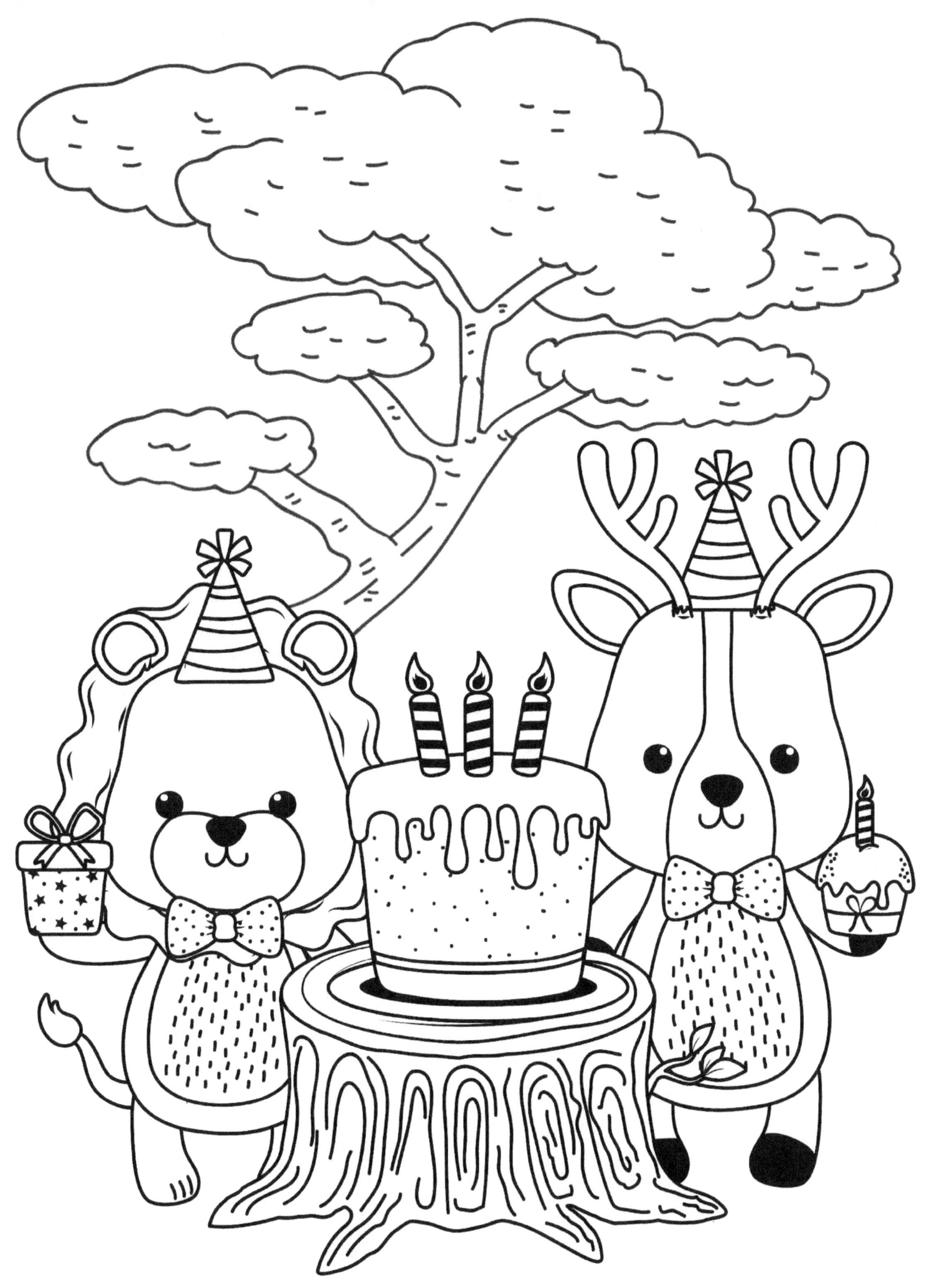

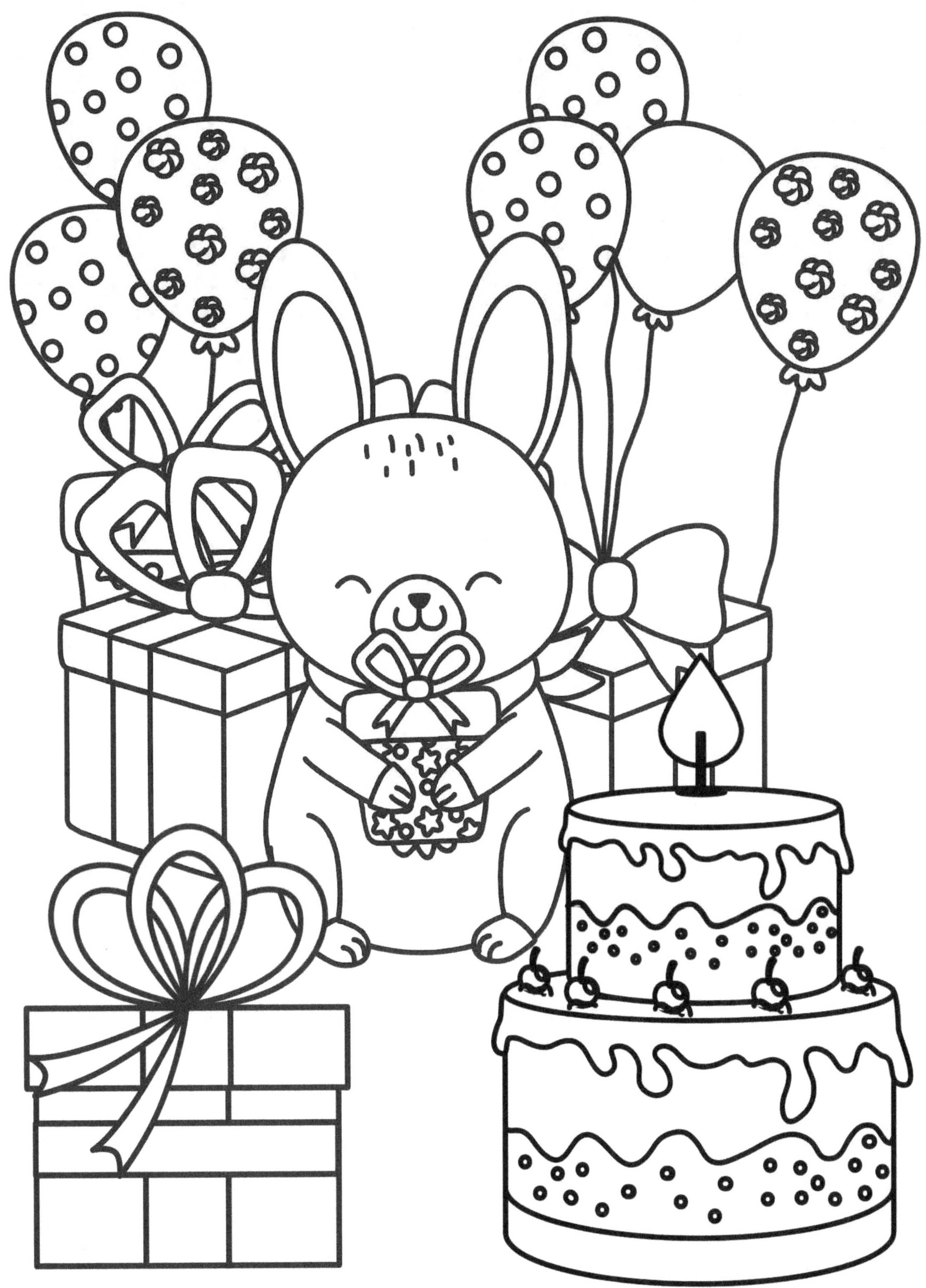

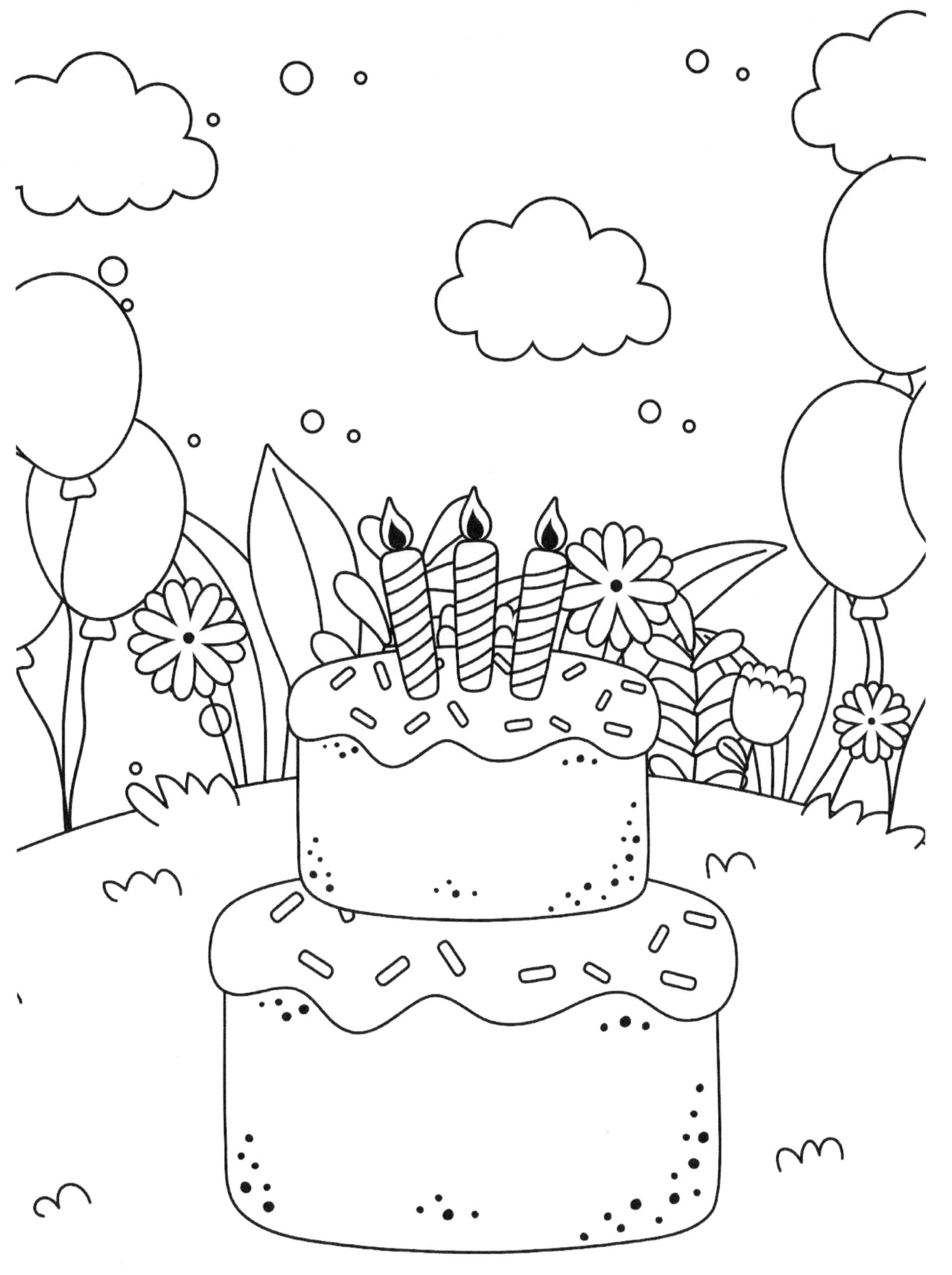

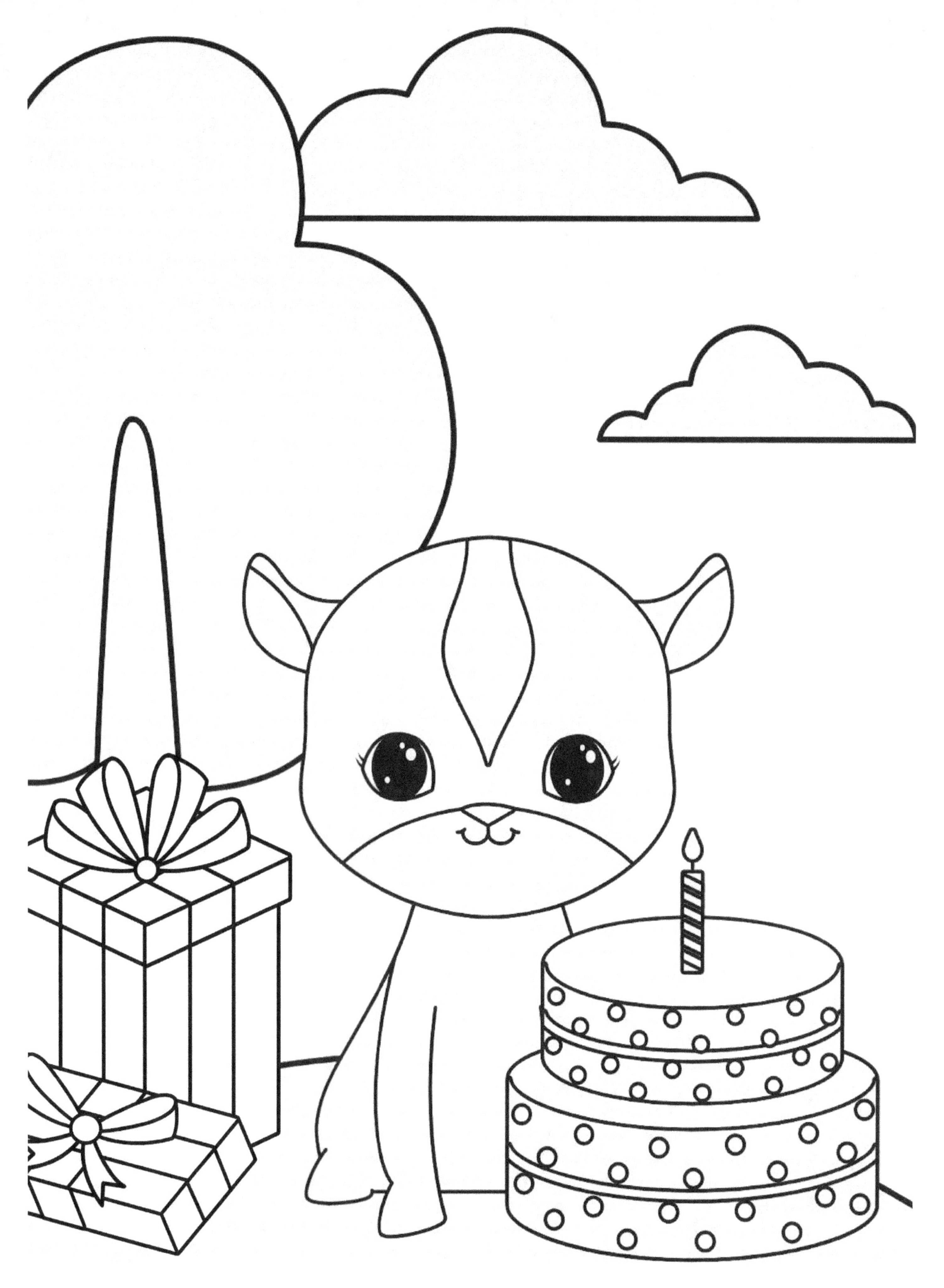

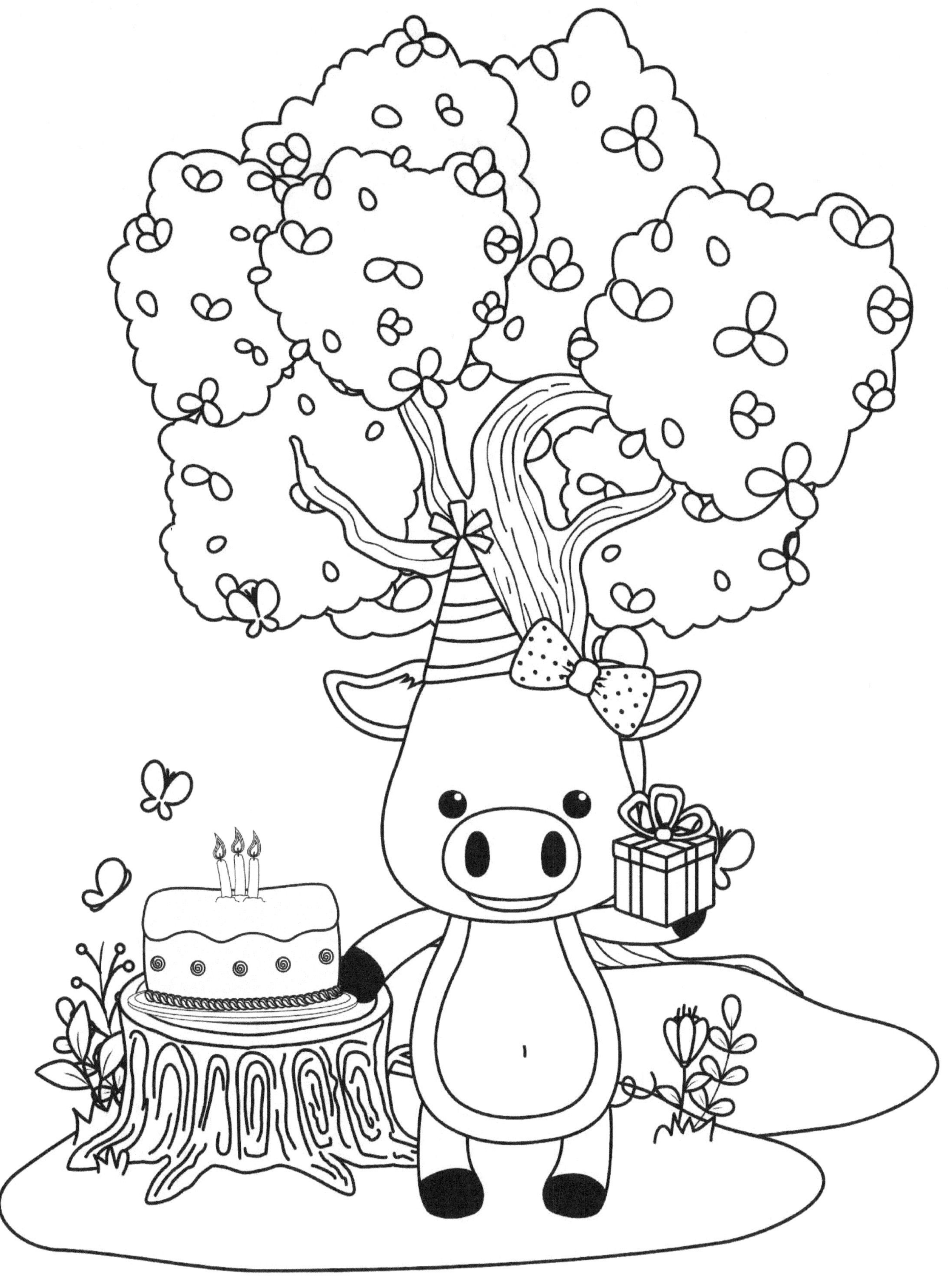

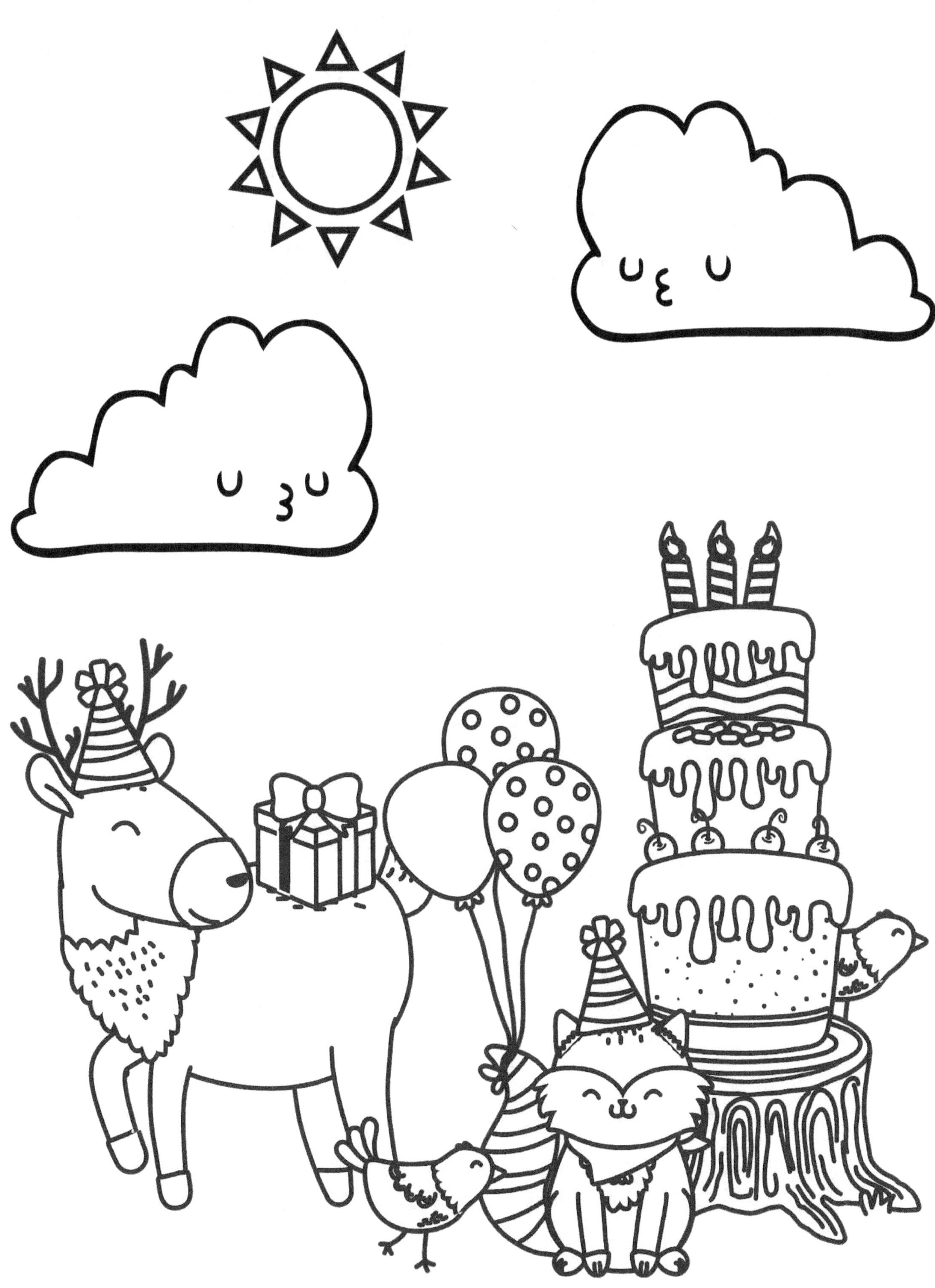

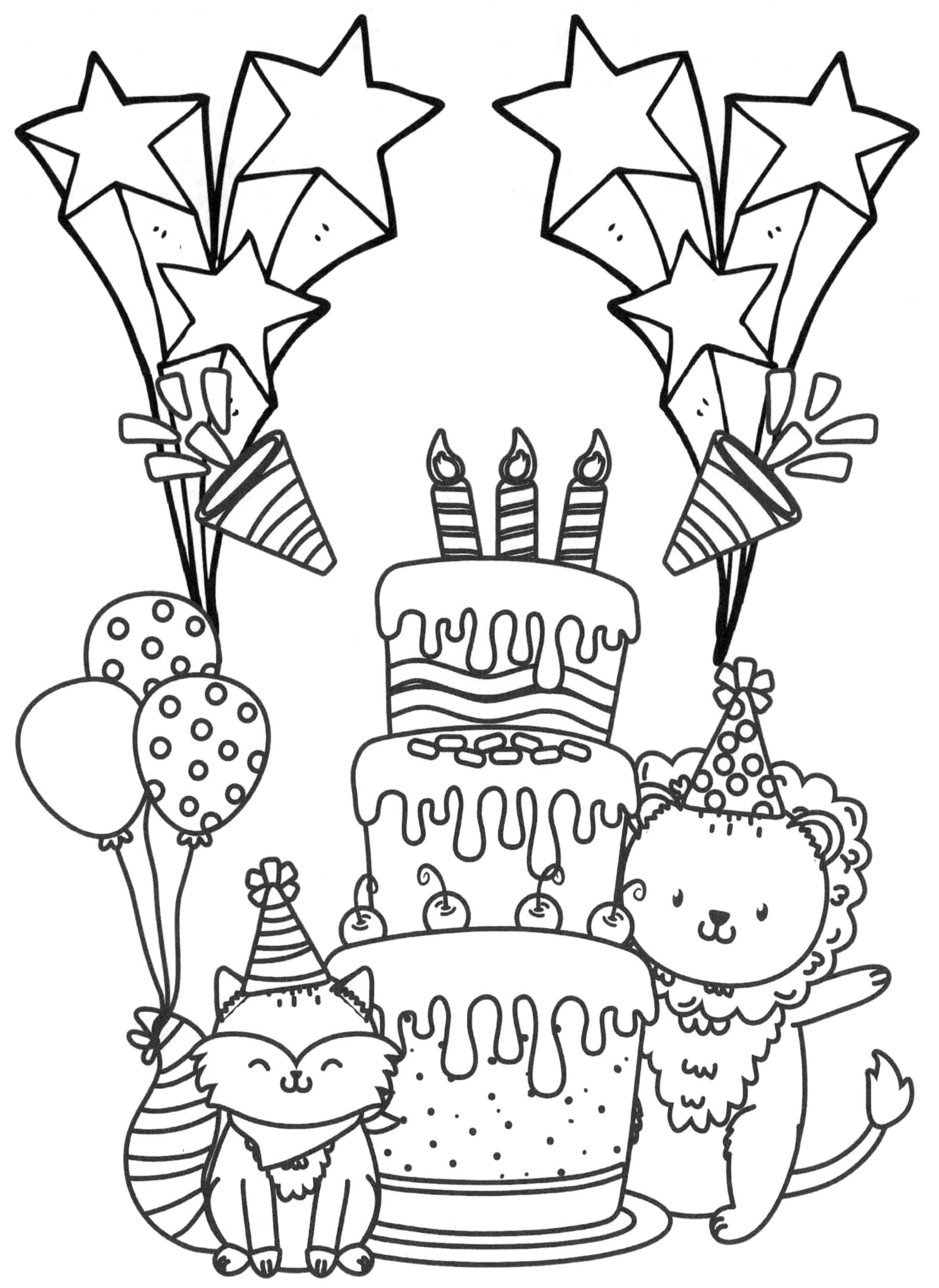

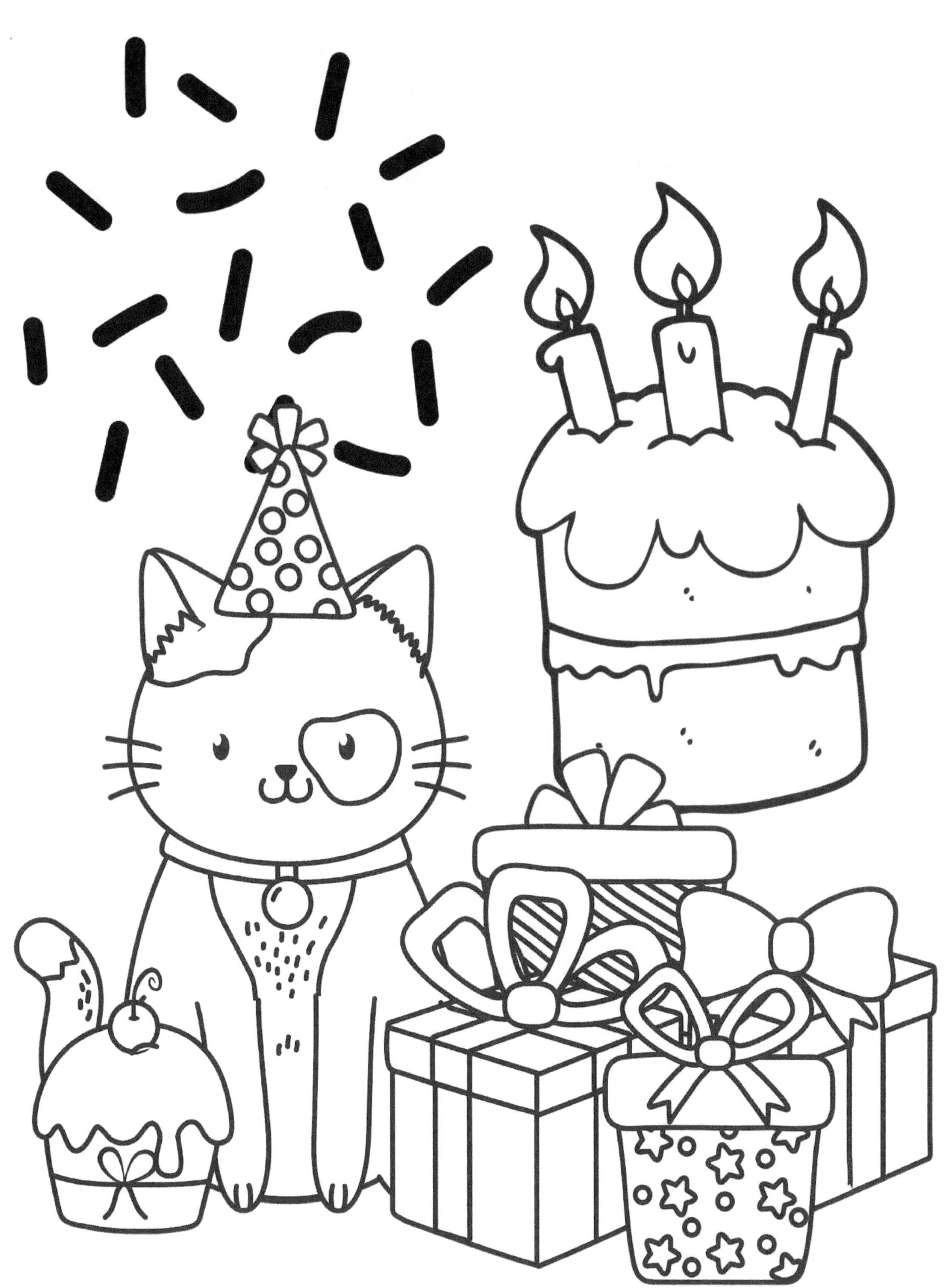

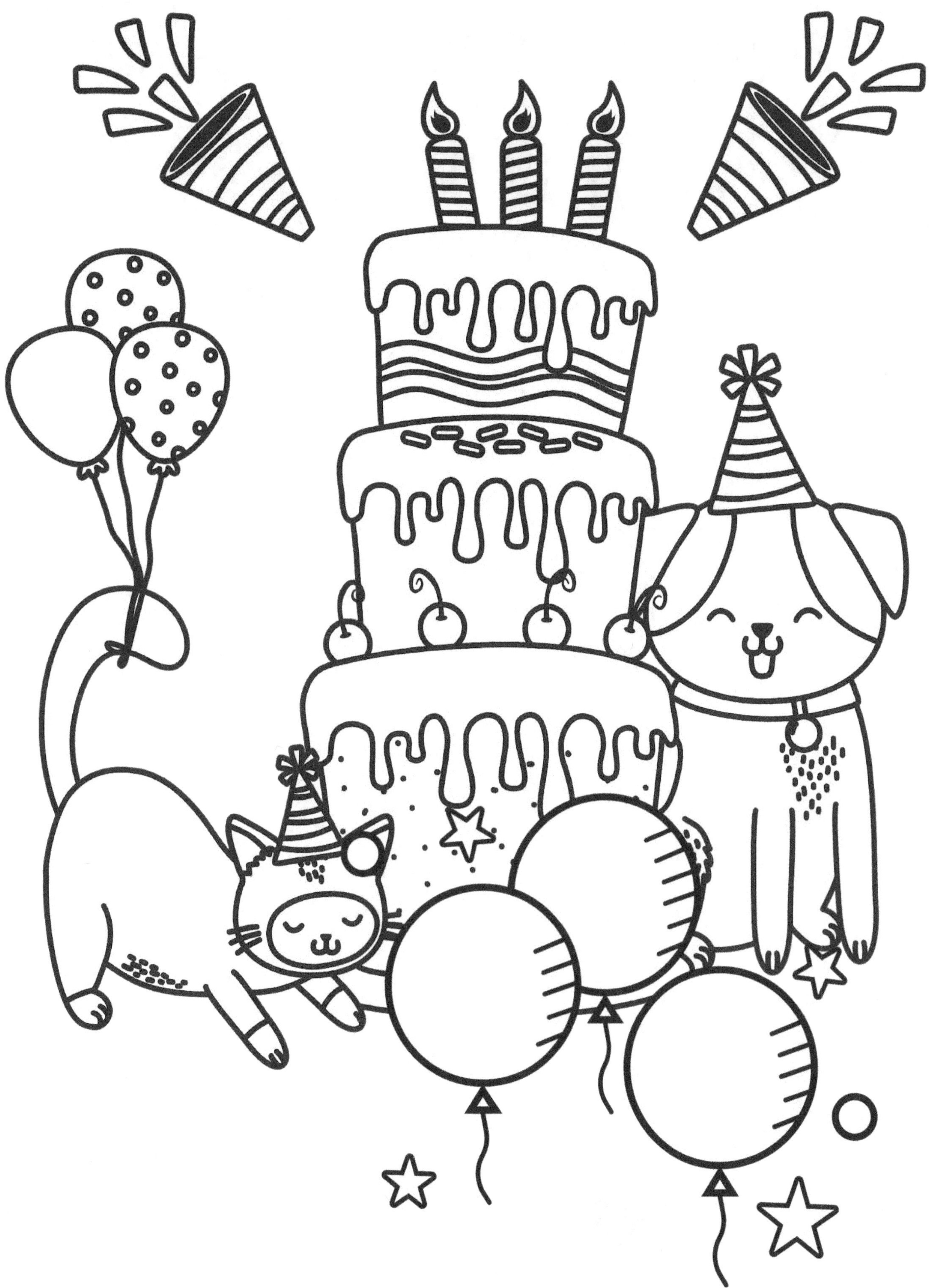

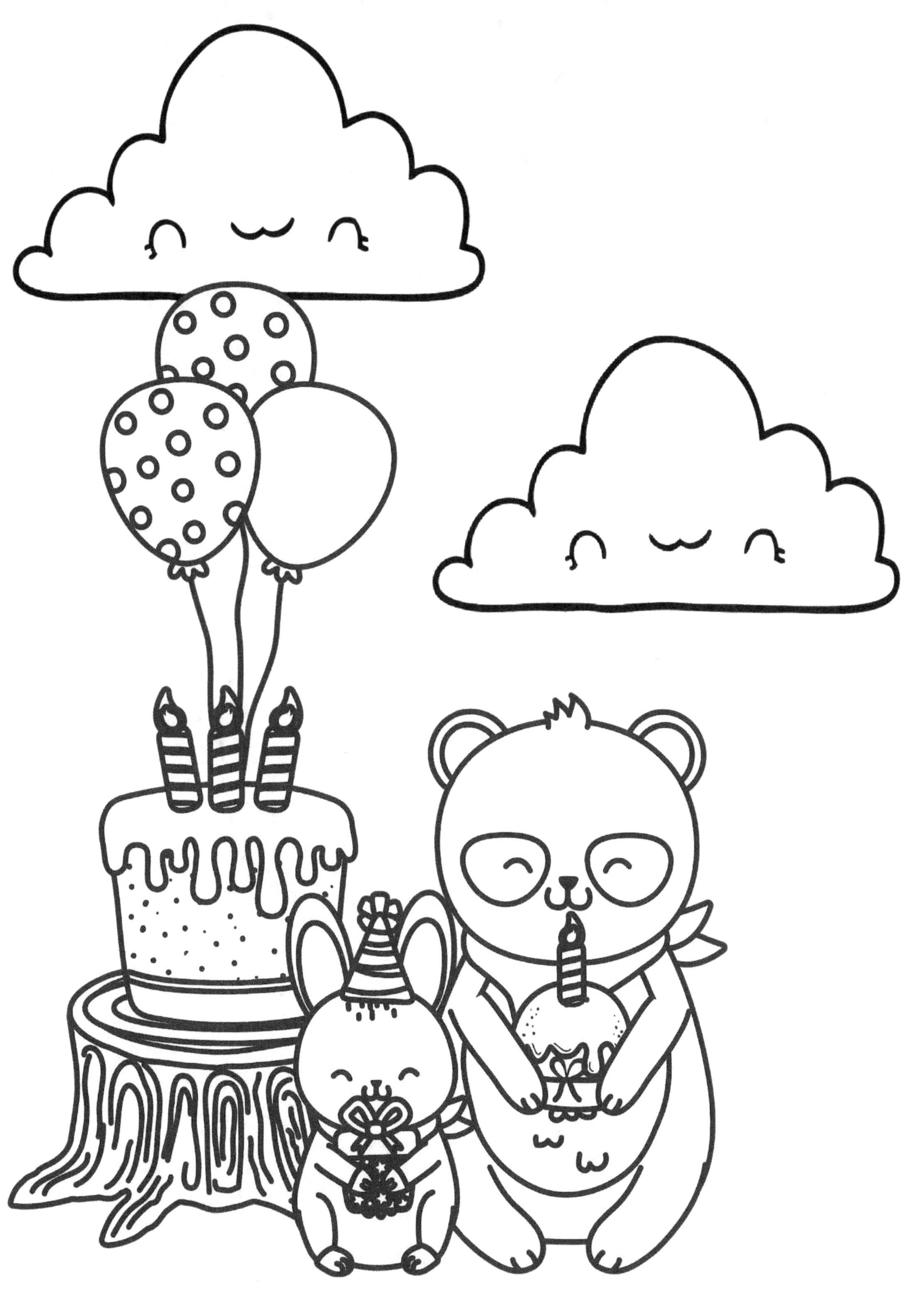

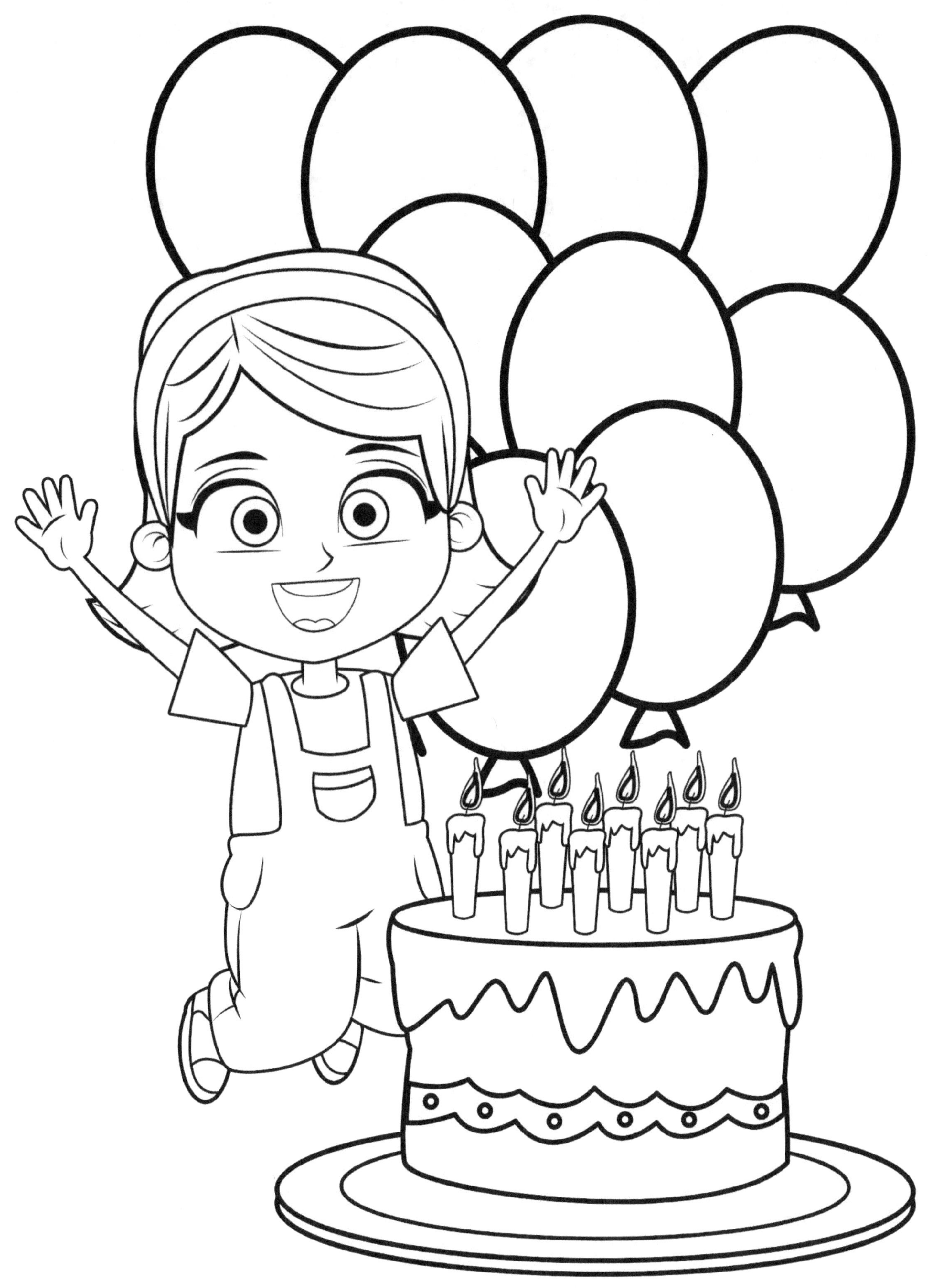

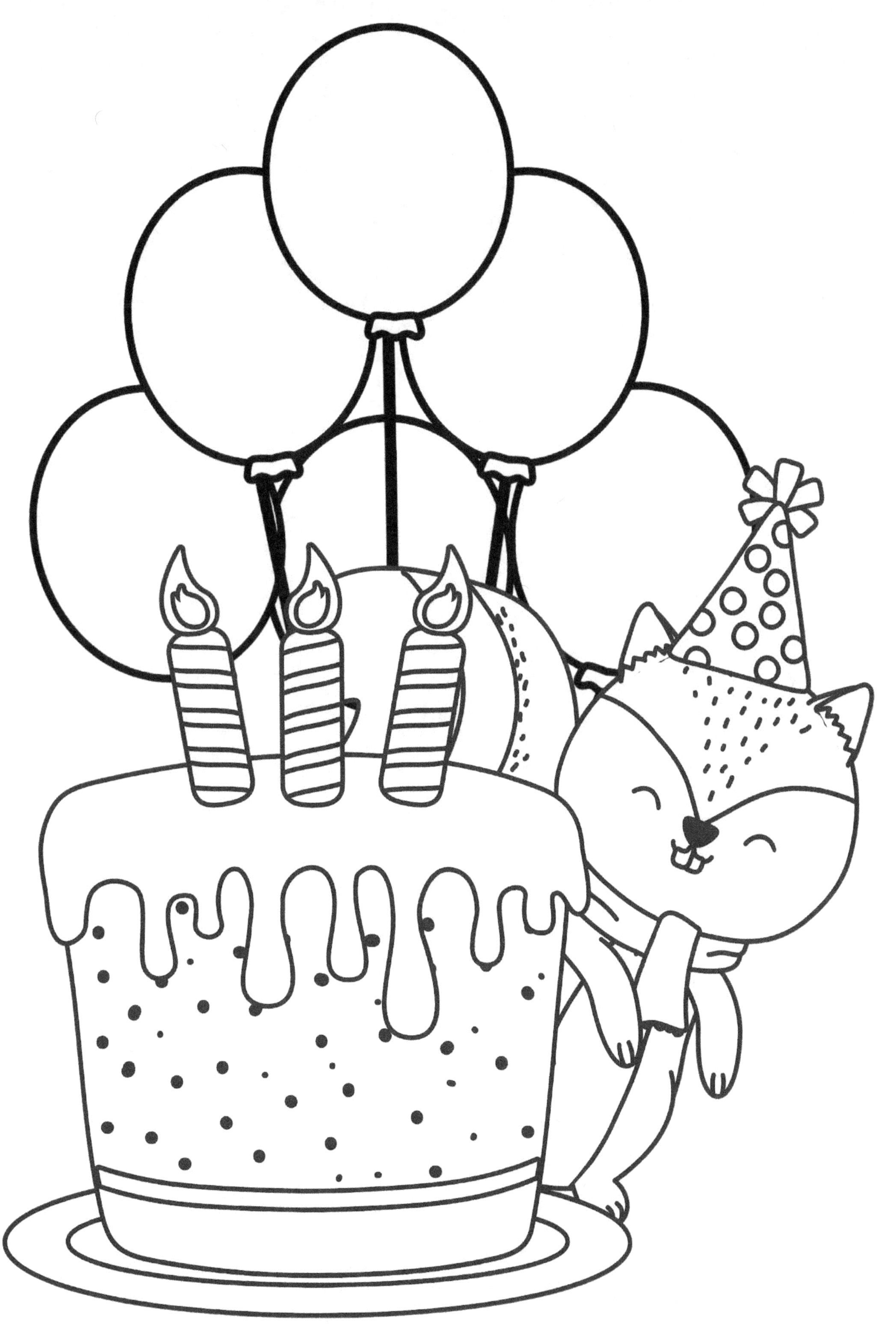

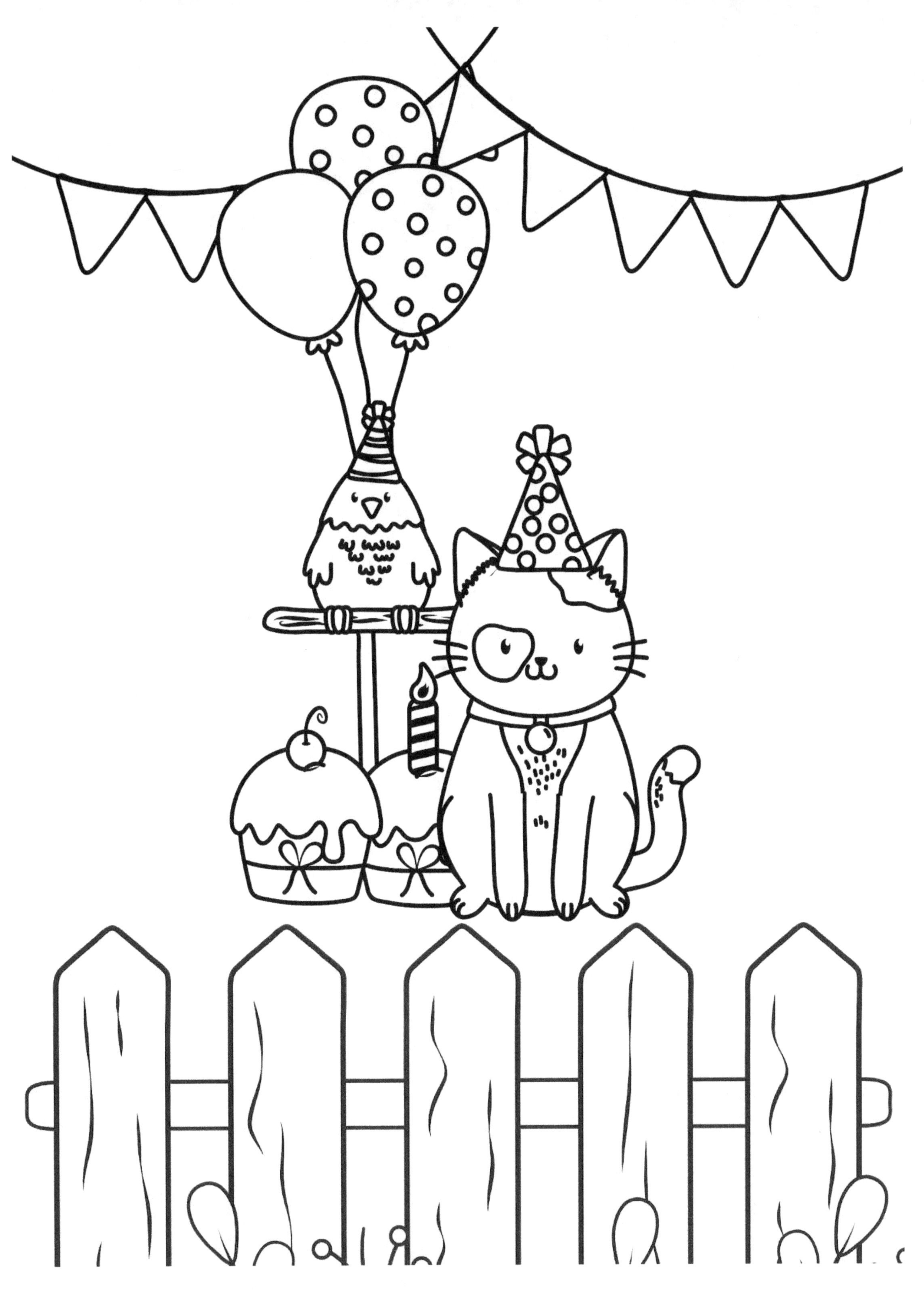

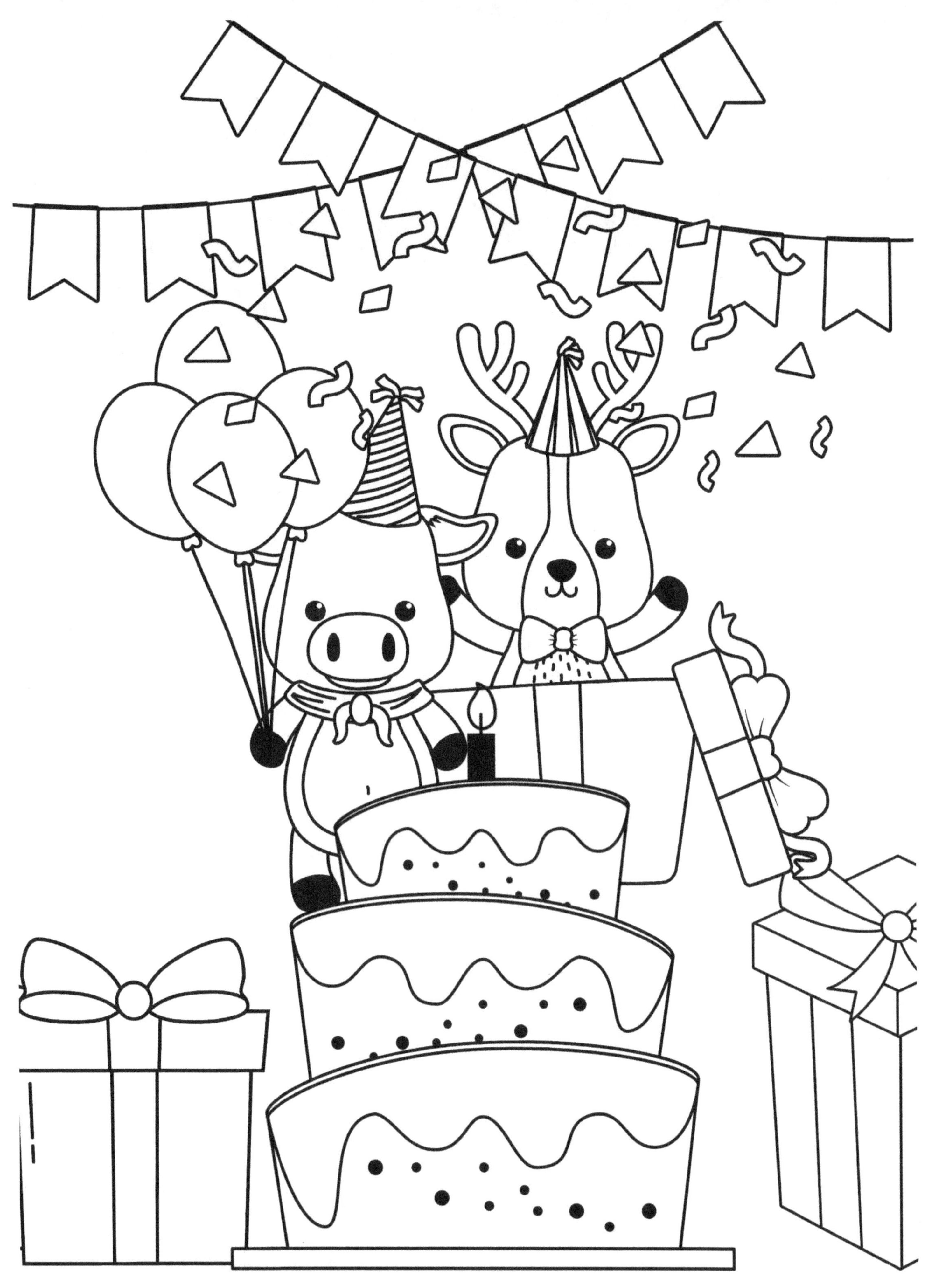

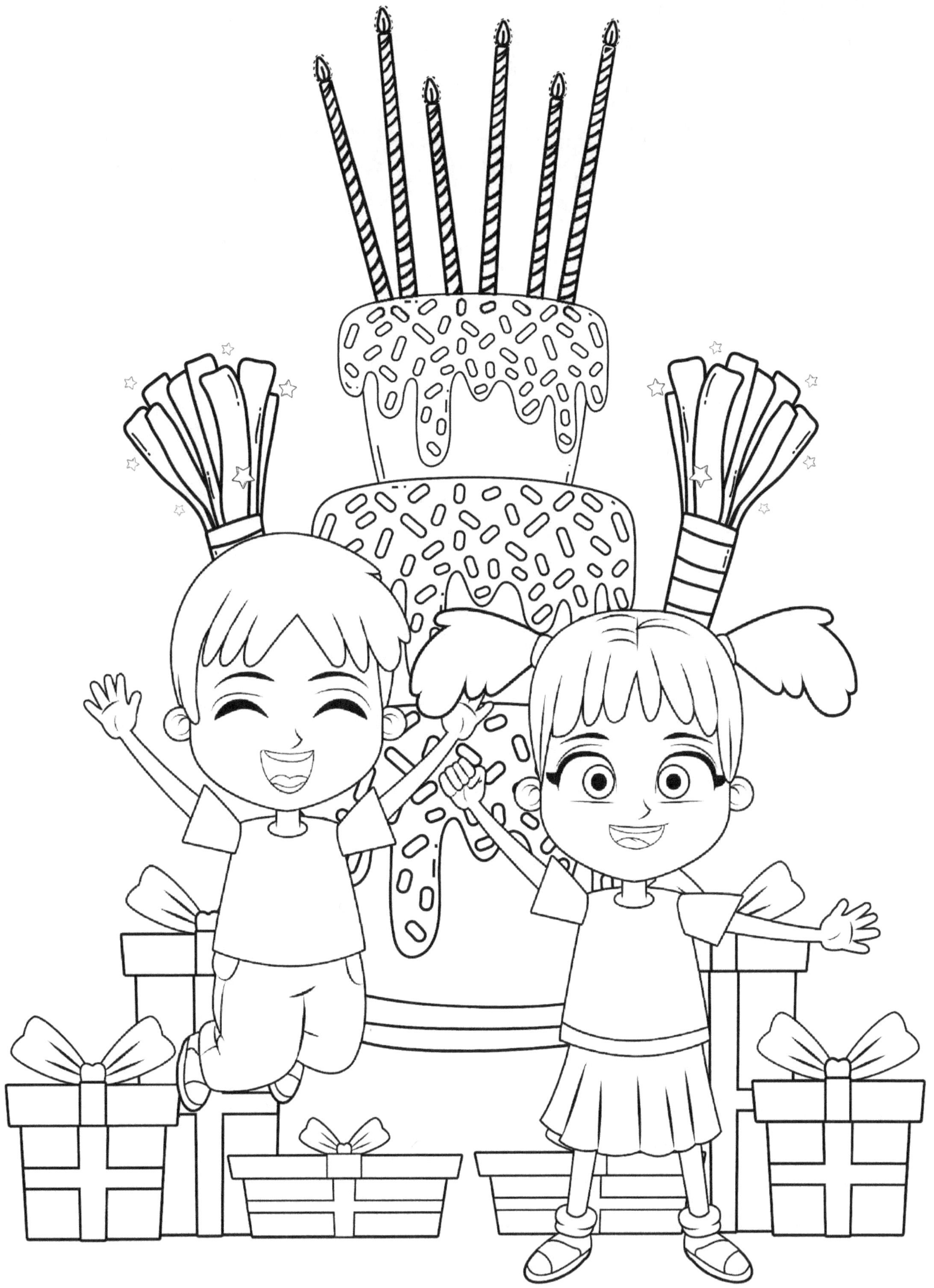

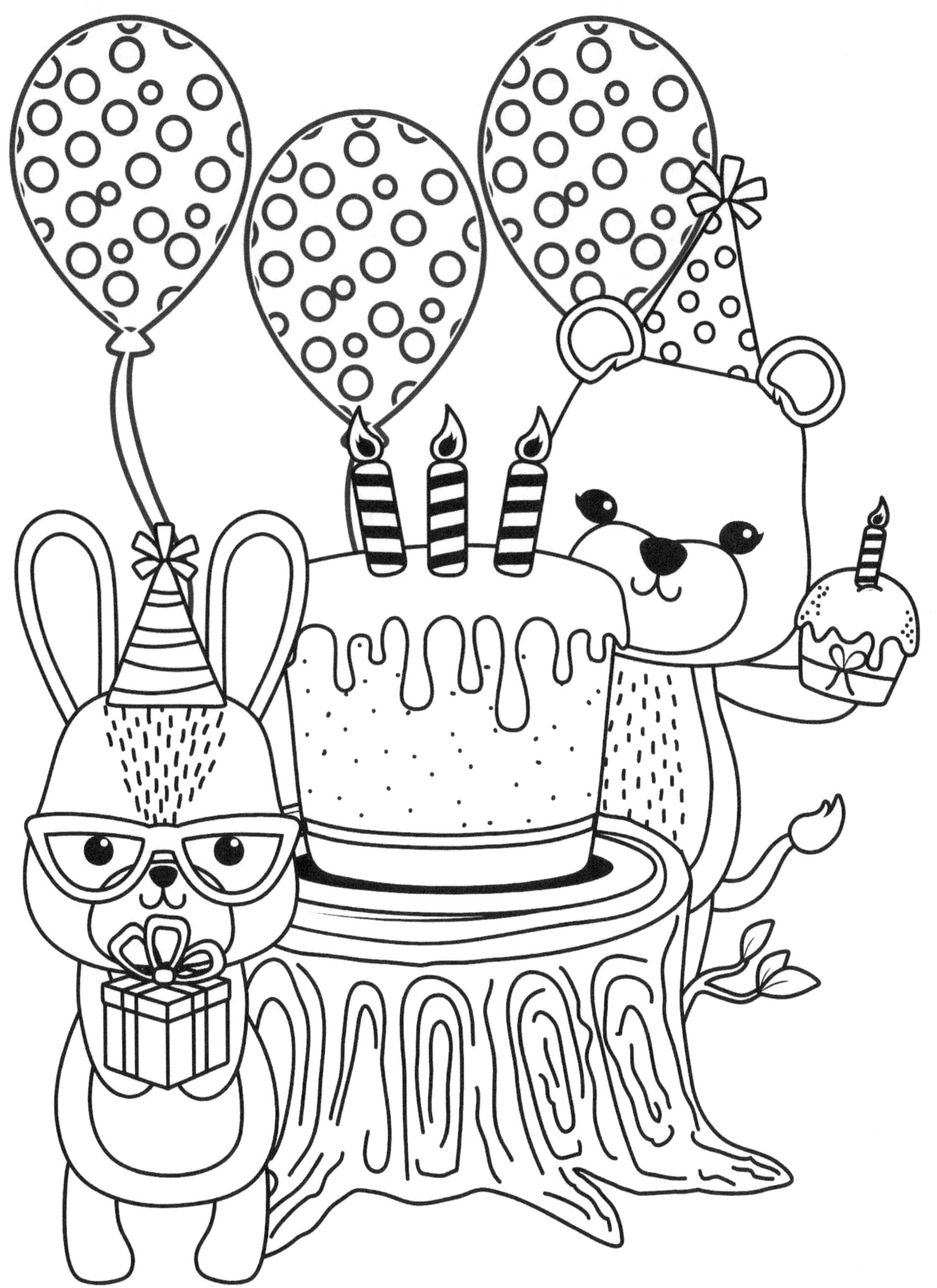

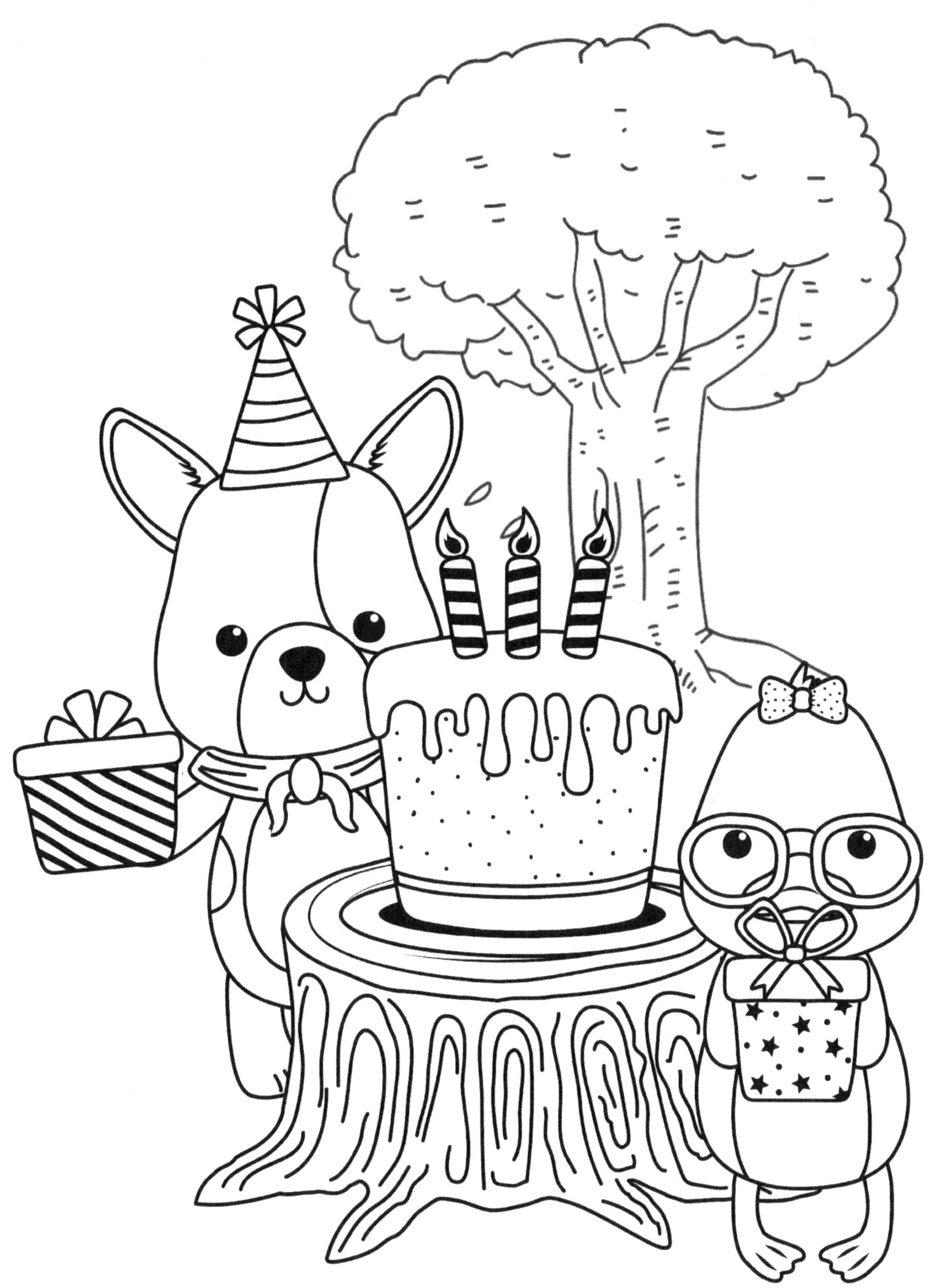

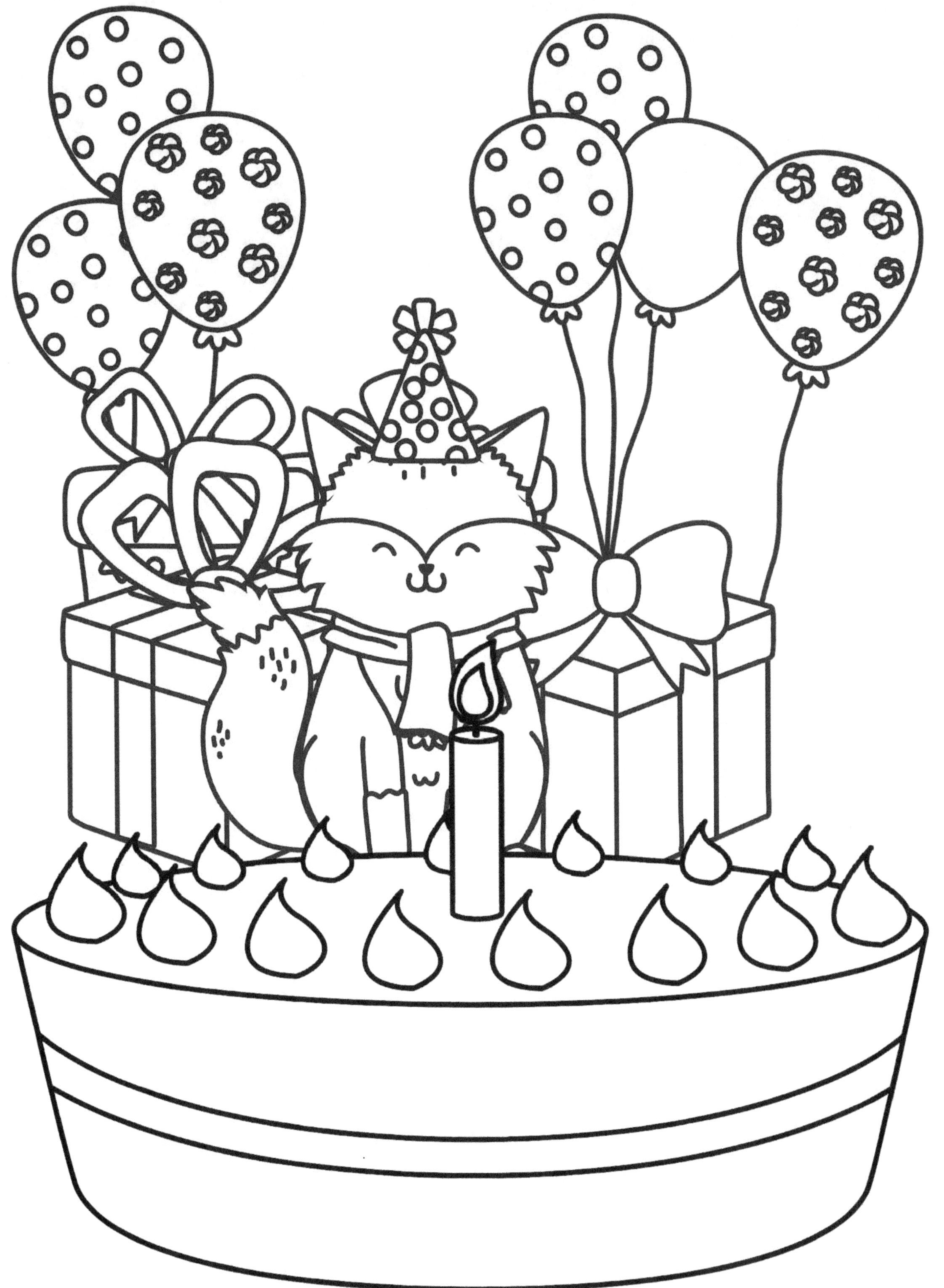

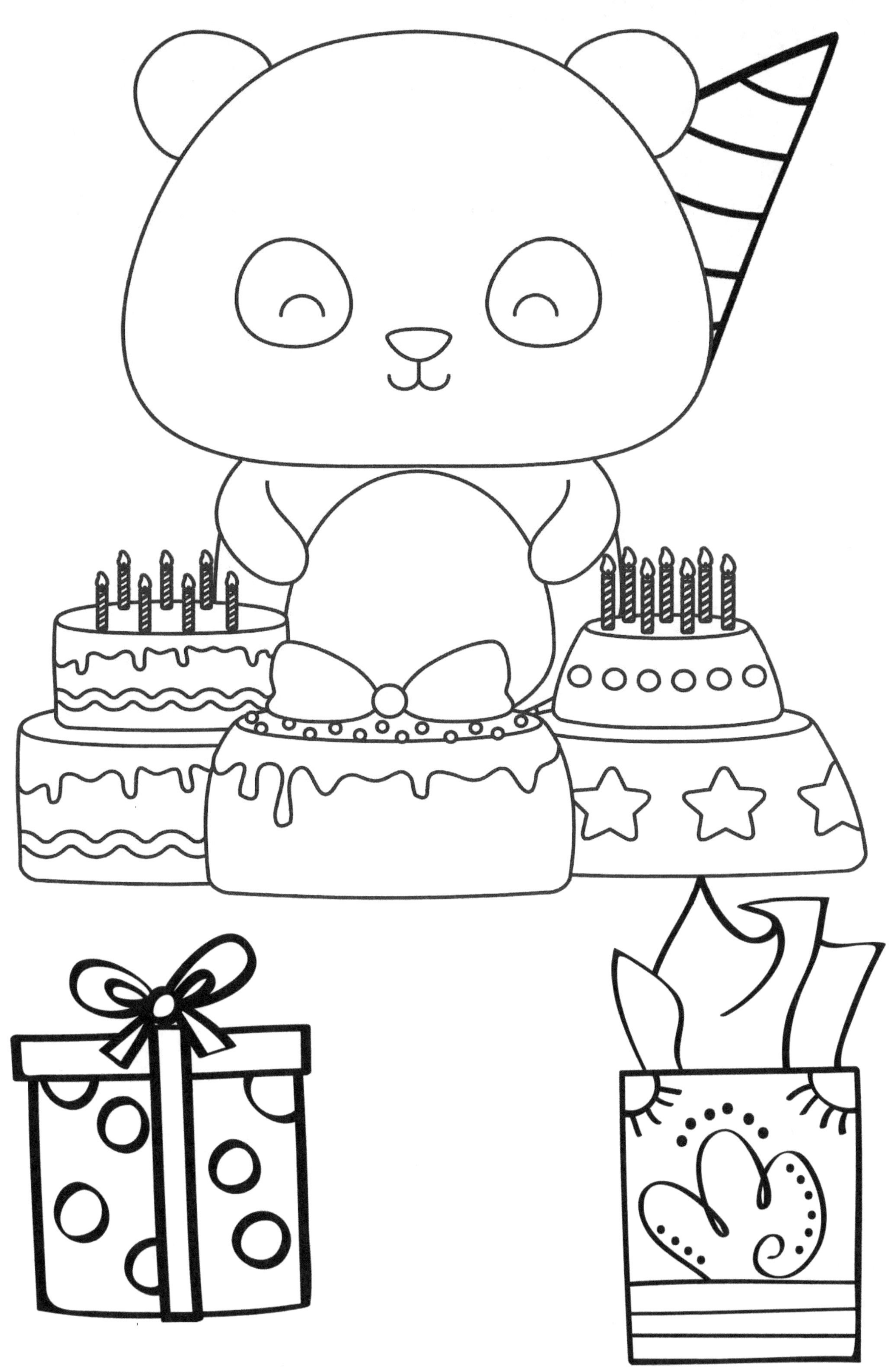

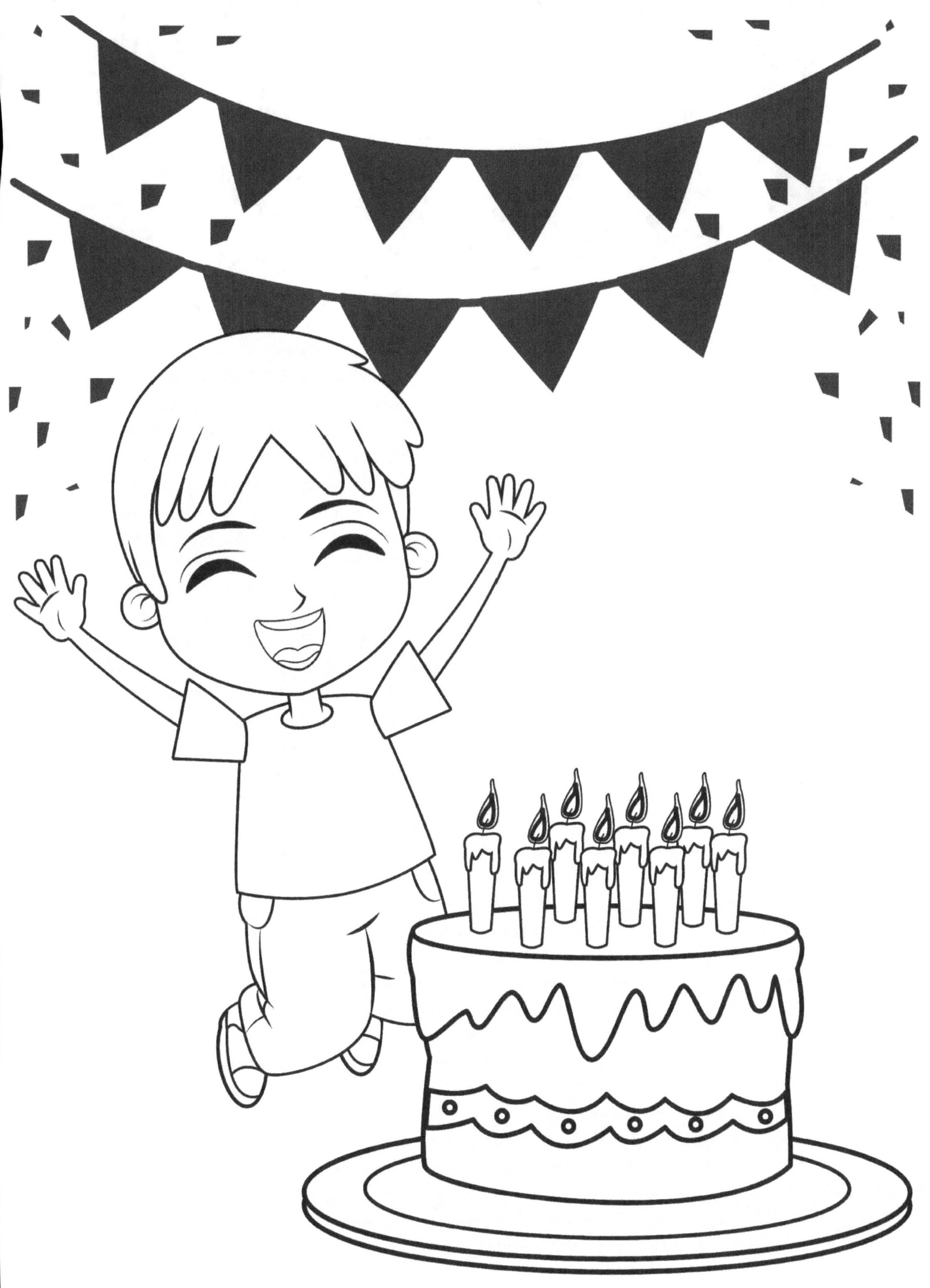

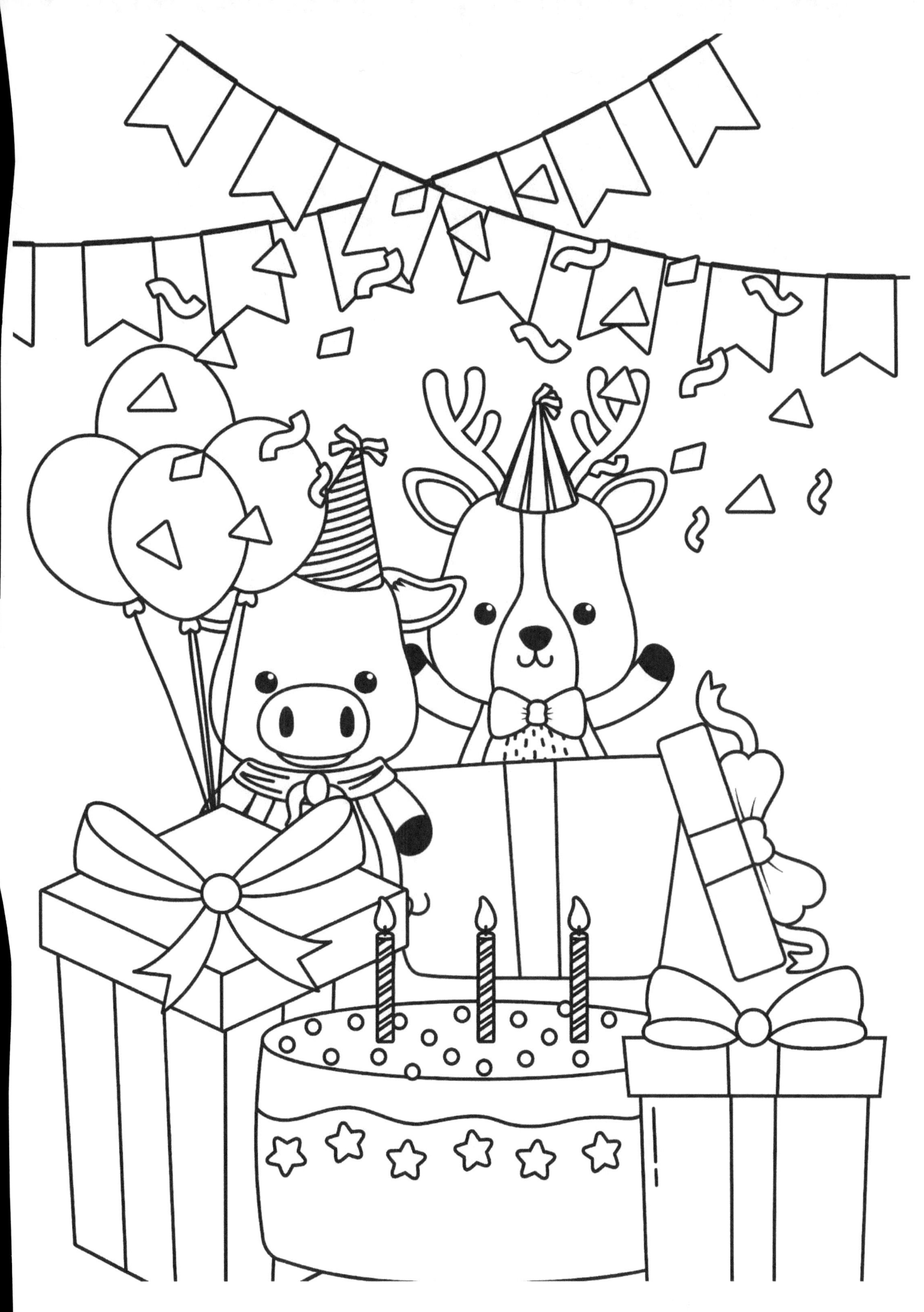